FROM THE NATIONAL HOUSE OF PRAYER

JAMES

ESSENTIALS *for* EFFECTIVE PRAYER

BRAD FIDLER

FOREWORD BY CHRIS BYBERG,
Executive Director of NHOP

JAMES: ESSENTIALS FOR EFFECTIVE PRAYER
Copyright © 2024 by Brad Fidler
Cover concept by Aaron MacDonald

All rights reserved. Neither this publication nor any part of this publication may be reproduced or transmitted in any form or by any means, electronic or mechanical, including photocopying, recording or any information storage and retrieval system, without permission in writing from the author.

Unless otherwise indicated, all scripture quotations are from the ESV® Bible (The Holy Bible, English Standard Version®), © 2001 by Crossway, a publishing ministry of Good News Publishers. Used by permission. All rights reserved. The ESV text may not be quoted in any publication made available to the public by a Creative Commons license. The ESV may not be translated in whole or in part into any other language. Scripture marked (NKJV) taken from the New King James Version®. Copyright © 1982 by Thomas Nelson. Used by permission. All rights reserved. Scripture quotations marked (NIV) are taken from the Holy Bible, New International Version®, NIV®. Copyright © 1973, 1978, 1984, 2011 by Biblica, Inc.™ Used by permission of Zondervan. All rights reserved worldwide. www.zondervan.com The "NIV" and "New International Version" are trademarks registered in the United States Patent and Trademark Office by Biblica, Inc.™ Scripture quotations marked (NLT) are taken from the Holy Bible, New Living Translation, copyright ©1996, 2004, 2015 by Tyndale House Foundation. Used by permission of Tyndale House Publishers, a Division of Tyndale House Ministries, Carol Stream, Illinois 60188. All rights reserved. Scripture quotations taken from the (NASB®) New American Standard Bible®, Copyright © 1960, 1971, 1977, 1995, 2020 by The Lockman Foundation. Used by permission. All rights reserved. lockman.org Scripture quotations taken from the Amplified® Bible (AMP), Copyright © 2015 by The Lockman Foundation. Used by permission. lockman.org

ISBN: 978-1-4866-2579-6
eBook ISBN: 978-1-4866-2580-2

Word Alive Press
119 De Baets Street Winnipeg, MB R2J 3R9
www.wordalivepress.ca

Cataloguing in Publication information can be obtained from Library and Archives Canada.

To Chris and Marilyn.

To say I would never have written this book
if it weren't for you is an understatement.
You have shaped my life in so many ways. I would not be who I am
today without your influence in my life. Thank you for everything.

CONTENTS

ACKNOWLEDGEMENTS	vii
FOREWORD	ix
INTRODUCTION Approaching James through the Lens of Prayer	1
ESSENTIAL #1 An Eternal Mindset (James 1:2–18)	11
ESSENTIAL #2 A Listening Heart in Prayer (James 1:19–26)	23
ESSENTIAL #3 Be Slow to Anger (James 1:19–20)	45
ESSENTIAL #4 Pray with Impartiality (James 2:1–13)	65
ESSENTIAL #5 Minister to the Poor (James 2:14–26)	77

ESSENTIAL #6
Freshwater Speech (James 3:1–12)   91

ESSENTIAL #7
Heavenly Wisdom (James 3:13–18)   111

ESSENTIAL #8
Humility (James 4:1—5:12)   135

ESSENTIAL #9
Fervent and Righteous (James 5:13–20)   155

APPENDIX A
Main Points and Prayer Points   179

APPENDIX B
NHOP and the Canopy of Prayer   189

ACKNOWLEDGEMENTS

Melissa, Joel, Owen, and Lukas—thank you for making space for me to take a shot at this, and for bearing with me through the ups and downs of the process. I love you guys.

Niagara Community Church—thank you for making space for me to work with the National House of Prayer. You are all wonderful examples of selfless love, patient endurance, humility, and impartiality. I will be forever grateful for your generosity, encouragement, and confidence in me.

Gord, Paul, Michael, and Leo—thank you for challenging and encouraging me to write this. It was needed, and it is appreciated. It's been an honour to walk with you all.

The Tuesday morning NHOP Zoom prayer group—this book was born directly out of our weekly prayer times together. I love praying with people who pray the Word. Thank you all for your faithfulness and perseverance on the wall. "And your Father, who sees in secret, will reward you."

Paul, Uncle Marc, Kevin K., Mark, Janet, Gord, Kevin B., and Stephen—thank you for making time to read and provide your feedback. You've all served to sharpen not only some of my points, but my life. Thank you.

Aaron—you made this project come alive to me in a way I didn't see coming. You're brilliant. I really hope to do this with you again someday.

Rob and Fran—we barely know each other, but thank you again for pouring yourselves out on behalf of the Kingdom of God, and Canada. It's an honour to build on the foundation you two laid at the National House of Prayer.

FOREWORD

From the moment Brad entered our home for dinner twenty-six years ago, I sensed a special connection. I knew we would build the Kingdom together.

At fourteen, he was eager to learn and grow, and at thirty-seven I felt privileged to mentor him. Over the years, Brad proved to be an exceptional student and disciple, always ready to rise to any challenge presented. His talent as a worship leader blossomed in our youth group and eventually extended to Sunday mornings.

Watching him evolve into the lead elder at Niagara Community Church has been immensely gratifying. Our journey together exemplifies the power of mentorship and the transformative impact it can have on both mentor and mentee.

At the age of eighteen, recognizing Brad's exceptional academic prowess, I recommended that before embarking on his university journey he invest a year to fully devote himself to serving the Lord. Offering a few suggestions, he felt led to join IHOPKC. Over two years, he immersed himself in a fasted lifestyle, embracing the essence of the "one thing"—to behold the beauty of the Lord and understand the significance of night and day prayer and worship.

Brad has grown into a remarkable husband and father of three. Within his local church, he embodies a blend of strength and calm, serving as a dedicated leader. Moreover, his talents as a teacher shine through, as you'll discover in the pages of this book.

This book emerged during a challenging period for the Christian community in our nation. We noticed a recurring theme during our national Zoom calls at the National House of Prayer. It felt like our prayers were hitting a ceiling, as if they weren't fully heard.

Our posture of "Search me, O God" became pivotal. I found myself pondering what I might be doing wrong. Then echoes of James 3:11–12 began to resound within us: *"Can both fresh water and salt water flow from the same spring? My brothers and sisters, can a fig tree bear olives, or a grapevine bear figs?"* (NIV) It became clear that we couldn't bless and curse simultaneously; our language had to shift.

Amidst the upheaval of COVID, resisting the urge to curse governments and leaders was a daunting task. The question persisted: were we to be a source of freshwater or a spring contaminated with salt?

We began to realize that not only is James 3 significant, but the entire book serves as a guide for aligning our prayer lives—from James 1, where we learn that human anger doesn't achieve God's righteousness, to the understanding that faith without works is dead, not to mention our stance on caring for the poor and vulnerable, all the book's lessons are crucial.

Inspired by this, NHOP developed a prayer school curriculum centred around the book of James. It was from that foundation that I approached Brad to write this book.

I believe this book holds significance because it emphasizes the importance, especially at this moment, of aligning our focus with what truly matters to God. Frequently, we become entangled in matters that irritate or upset us, losing sight of what is truly significant. This book will confront your perspectives, ideally prompting a sense of repentance and guiding us to redirect our attention from trivialities toward the priorities that hold significance to God.

Within these pages, Brad skillfully captures the very essence of God's heart in prayer. It illuminates the significance of walking humbly and praying with a heart attuned to what matters to Him. Through its teachings, we discover the art of praying in alignment with His will and desires, rather than merely voicing our own opinions or grievances.

FOREWORD

This book serves as a guide, giving us practical principles to immerse ourselves deeply in the flow of God's presence. It shows us how to really swim in the river of God.

—Chris Byberg
Executive Director, National House of Prayer

INTRODUCTION

Approaching James through the Lens of Prayer

To the twelve tribes in the Dispersion...
(James 1:1)

As Christians, we love tracking with influential and anointed leaders: preachers, teachers, worship leaders, authors, and so on. We follow them on social media, buy their books and albums, and attend their conferences and concerts. The Lord uses them to encourage, challenge, inspire, and help us grow in our walk with Him. All good, right?

I think part of the reason we're drawn to these men and women of God is that we know a little bit about them. Maybe we're familiar with their testimony. Maybe we know about the local church or ministry they're part of and have heard stories of how God has moved in that ministry. We want to learn from them because we recognize how God is moving in their lives and we want the same for ourselves. Maybe they unpack the Scriptures in a way that we can really grasp. Maybe there's a tangible sense of the presence of God when we use their songs to worship. Or perhaps they provoke us to grow in prayer.

Whatever it is, we want to grow in the things they walk in.

I think the same goes for the biblical authors. We're pretty familiar with the backstories of people like Jesus, Moses, David, or Paul, because we're given lots of information about them. That might partially explain why the Gospels, the Torah, the Psalms, and Paul's epistles tend to get a little more attention than some of the other books.

But what about some of the lesser-known figures and their books? Would we take a greater interest in them if we knew a bit about these authors? Maybe you see where I'm going with this.

What do you know about James?

While we don't see James' story fully laid out like David's or Paul's, we are given little snippets here and there that shed some light on his unique life and journey.

The first thing to note is that this isn't the same James who appears throughout the Gospels as one of Jesus' inner circle disciples. That James was martyred by Herod in Acts 12:2. The James we're referring to was actually the half-brother of Jesus who later became an apostle and one of the pillars of the church in Jerusalem.

Let's start with this question: what was it like growing up as Jesus' little brother? At the age of twelve, Jesus was talking about God being His Father, so He had to be somewhat aware of His divinity (Luke 2:41–49). So what was it like for James to grow up in the same house as a boy who knew He was the God-Man? To share a childhood, to play, to compete? Maybe it was amazing; maybe it was awful.

I have three sons myself and know they don't always get along. They love each other, but at times they push each other's buttons. That almost always leads to conflict.

When something went wrong between Jesus and James, though, how often do you think Mary believed James' version of events over those of his big brother?

I imagine James' childhood wasn't all rosy. Though Jesus was his own flesh and blood, James wasn't initially a believer. John 7:5 tells us that not even Jesus' own brothers believed in Him. Maybe that shouldn't be surprising. James knew better than anyone that Jesus was fully man; it must have been a stretch to believe that He was also fully God. He may have found the idea downright offensive!

This seems possible when we consider that wider passage in John 7. The chapter begins with an acknowledgement that Jesus was avoiding the region of Judea, because it was known that the Jews there sought to kill Him. Then we read that Jesus' own brothers challenged Him to go to Judea, perhaps from a place of scepticism: "If you're really the Messiah, you wouldn't keep it hidden. Go and do your miracles there and show the world who you are" (John 7:3–4, paraphrased). Sounds like they tried to get Him into a hostile situation by challenging His ego.

However you slice it, the passage seems to indicate that Jesus' brothers weren't entirely friendly with Him.

Whether or not there were challenges, one thing I imagine James witnessed in those hidden days was the formation of Jesus' prayer life. We see throughout the Gospels that Jesus regularly retreated to solitary places to pray. He constantly made time and space to come before His Father in the secret place. A habit like that doesn't magically spring up when a public ministry starts. No, it's cultivated long before then.

I'm willing to bet that James often saw Jesus slip off to be alone. Maybe Jesus told him why, maybe not, but I bet James noticed something going on.

James grew up in the same house as Jesus, witnessing firsthand His thirty-year season of obscurity not revealed to us in Scripture. He watched Jesus cultivate the prayer life that would become the lifeline of the most powerfully supernatural ministry in human history.

Do you think he might have anything useful to teach us about prayer?

Though James' heart may have initially been stuck in the tumult of sibling rivalry, Jesus wasn't offended or dissuaded. He was very patient with James. He never wrote him off.

We know this because of Jesus' actions after His resurrection. Paul details these events for us in 1 Corinthians 15. After appearing to Mary Magdalene, Jesus visited Peter and then the twelve disciples together. Then He appeared to more than five hundred believers all at once.

At last Paul makes a beautiful little statement: *"Then he appeared to James..."* (1 Corinthians 15:7).

It's easy to miss the weight of that line. Jesus made a point to pay a very personal visit to His unbelieving brother. To be rejected by man is painful. To be rejected by your hometown? That's personal. But to be rejected by a brother? Few things could hurt as deeply.

But Jesus went to this brother who had rejected Him, appearing to him in His resurrected glory. Jesus gave James another chance, and another reason, to believe.

I think it's safe to say that this encounter marked James in a significant way. He went from doubting Jesus' claims to being a leader of

His church in Jerusalem—in a time of intense persecution, no less. He remained with the believers in Jerusalem even as persecution exploded in the aftermath of Stephen's martyrdom. James was no fair-weather believer; by this time, he was as fiercely loyal to the Lord Jesus as anyone.

James also developed a prayer life of his own. A strong prayer life. Early church tradition tells us that he earned the nickname Old Camel Knees because he developed heavy callouses on his knees from his long hours in prayer. Think about that: his prayer life literally altered his physical appearance.

Yes, Jesus' post-resurrection visit with James radically altered the course of his life. James had missed out on walking with Jesus in the days of His earthly ministry, but he seized the opportunity to abide with Him in the place of prayer after He had ascended. James became a prolific man of prayer.

This is the man who wrote the book of James.

Again, do you think he might have some things to teach us about prayer?

James is a remarkable book. It covers a lot of ground in just five short chapters. It's amazingly pointed in its instruction for a book that's considered a "general epistle." It's plain to see his encouragements for how to live well with one another, but there's an undeniable undercurrent of prayer through it all.

Before we dive into the meat of this letter, I want to be clear about how we're going to approach it for the purpose of this book.

WHERE I'M COMING FROM

The National House of Prayer (NHOP) exists to activate strategic prayer across Canada. It was founded by Rob and Fran Parker in 2004 to be an embassy for God in our nation's capital, Ottawa. For approximately fifteen years, believers from across the country gathered at NHOP's building, mere blocks from Parliament Hill, to pray, meet their elected officials, and get a better understanding of how our government works so they could pray focused prayers that hit the mark.

Central to our purpose as a ministry is 1 Timothy 2:1–4:

> First of all, then, I urge that supplications, prayers, intercessions, and thanksgivings be made for all people, for kings and all who are in high positions, that we may lead a peaceful and quiet life, godly and dignified in every way. This is good, and it is pleasing in the sight of God our Savior, who desires all people to be saved and to come to the knowledge of the truth.

Since 2020, NHOP has undergone a shift in how we function. Rather than focusing on calling people to Ottawa to pray, we are raising up prayer teams in every electoral riding across Canada to cover churches, communities, and constituencies (municipal, provincial, and federal) with prayer. We call it the Canopy of Prayer. We're here to inspire, encourage, and equip people to pray. We do this by hosting weekly national prayer calls, hosting and traveling to speak at conferences and prayer intensives, and through our School of Prayer.

This book is the result of a class we taught in that School of Prayer, looking at how the content of James applies to prayer. What we saw in this epistle has radically impacted how we pray. As we shared those learnings, we received similar feedback from those who took the class: James was altering the way they prayed. One participant told us, "I feel like I finally know how to pray." This feedback didn't come from brand-new believers, but from people of prayer who had walked with the Lord for decades.

We believe that the Holy Spirit is emphasizing the themes in this book to the church in Canada today. These themes relate not only to how we pray, but how we can live in such a way as to enhance our prayer lives instead of hindering them.

THE LETTER ITSELF

While there is some debate about the authorship, it's widely accepted that the letter's author is James, the brother of Jesus. He was the first bishop of the church in Jerusalem and a key figure at the Jerusalem council in Acts 15. We've already mentioned his nickname, Old Camel

Knees, which speaks to his devout prayer life, but he was also known as James the Just. This speaks to his renowned piety. Just as his heart for prayer bleeds through his words, we can also see his heart for justice.

James addressed his epistle to *"the twelve tribes in the Dispersion"* (James 1:1). This means that he was addressing a very broad audience.

Many epistles were written to churches in specific cities like Ephesus, Rome, or Corinth. Some were written to the church in one city but recommended to be distributed to others within the region, such as the letter to the Colossians. Some were written to specific leaders, like Timothy and Titus. Many of these letters addressed specific problems or situations, providing focused teaching designed to speak to those issues.

But James cast a much broader net. He wrote to all the believers scattered throughout the known world, who at the time were predominantly Jewish.

After the martyrdom of Stephen in Acts 8, there was an explosion of persecution against the believers in Jerusalem, and they began to spread outward. Jesus had told them they would be His witnesses *"in Jerusalem and in all Judea and Samaria, and to the end of the earth"* (Acts 1:8), but they likely hadn't imagined they would be sent out in this way. Many of them ran for their lives, moving first into Judea and Samaria, and eventually beyond.

By the time James wrote this letter, these mostly Jewish believers were scattered throughout the Roman Empire.

No distinction is made in terms of who among the believers this letter was intended for. It wasn't addressed to specific leaders, elders, or individuals.

This means it spoke to all believers. It applied to the young as much as to the old, to the believer who was saved on the day of Pentecost as much as the believer who joined the church the week before this letter arrived. It applied to elders and deacons as much as those entrusted to their care. It applied to the ones who functioned in more public gifts—like prophecy, healings, miracles, interpretation of tongues, etc.—and it applied to those with gifts that tend to operate behind the scenes—such as administration, helps, mercy, hospitality, etc.

INTRODUCTION: APPROACHING JAMES *through the* LENS *of* PRAYER

The bottom line is that this letter applies to every believer, no matter their maturity in Christ, season of life, gift mix, role, or function within the body. In the same way, it applies to every one of us today.

James touches on several themes in his letter, such as endurance, double-mindedness, the rich and poor, and being doers of the Word. He revisits several of them, giving us an indication of their importance. Prayer is one such theme that Old Camel Knees repeatedly touches on.

Three times, James directly comments on prayer. What's really interesting is how he specifically addresses the effectiveness of our prayers each time. In James 1, while urging the believers to seek God for wisdom, he says that the one who prays while doubting *"must not suppose that he will receive anything from the Lord"* (James 1:7). In James 4, he writes that the result of asking from a wrong motive is unanswered prayer (James 4:3). And at the close of the book, we come to one of the most oft-quoted prayer verses: *"The effective, fervent prayer of a righteous man avails much"* (James 5:16, NKJV).

In these three statements, James comments twice on the causes of ineffective prayer, and once on effective prayer. Think about it: James gave us some parameters for an effective prayer life!

The prevailing understanding of prayer in the West is that it is a verbal exercise: we voice our thoughts, concerns, joys, struggles, petitions, and requests to God… and that's generally it.

If that's the extent of your definition of prayer, it can be easy to find yourself wondering how to find the right mix of words, a sort of magic formula, to get God to answer. If you think about it, that boils down to a sort of control or manipulation: "I did or said ABC, now You must do XYZ."

But that thinking runs contrary to the gospel of grace: *"For by grace you have been saved through faith. And this is not your own doing; it is the gift of God, <u>not a result of works, so that no one may boast</u>"* (Ephesians 2:8–9, emphasis added).

In Romans 4, Paul points out that to the one who works, wages aren't considered a gift but their rightful due (Romans 4:4). This thinking shows up when we have the attitude that God owes us something or exists primarily to benefit us.

You may be thinking, "Those verses apply to salvation. We're talking about prayer here." True. But the heart of Paul's message to the Galatians is that we aren't just saved by grace. Indeed, the entire working out of our Christian lives is done through the grace of God. He writes,

> Let me ask you only this: Did you receive the Spirit by works of the law or by hearing with faith? Are you so foolish? *Having begun by the Spirit, are you now being perfected by the flesh?* …Does he who supplies the Spirit to you and works miracles among you do so by works of the law, or by hearing with faith… (Galatians 3:2–5, emphasis added)

In the same way, we can perform no works to force God's hand in answering our prayers. There is no clever mix of words, no secret formula, no silver bullet. In fact, when our focus in prayer is on getting what we want, James tells us, *"You ask amiss"* (James 4:3, NKJV). Prayer is not a tool we use to get God to do stuff for us. Nor is He looking for polished stanzas that will impress Him to the point of twisting His arm into action.

Rather, prayer is the communicative encapsulation of a pleasing life and worthy walk before Him. Our character and the motives of our heart affect prayer. After all, James did say that it is the prayer of a *righteous person* that is effective (James 5:16).

Having said all this, please understand that we're going to look at James specifically as it relates to prayer and how these instructions and truths apply to our prayer lives. I'm not saying that James was primarily writing this letter to address how to maintain our prayer lives, but it certainly is one of his intended themes. This letter was written to address the whole of the Christian life, and James seems to suggest that the whole of the Christian life affects our prayers.

That's the heart of what this book is about.

James' instructions are timely for the praying church today. Western culture has shifted radically in the past twenty years, and those winds of change only appear to be increasing in strength and speed. Differing

INTRODUCTION: APPROACHING JAMES *through the* LENS *of* PRAYER

views and ideologies have morphed into battlelines drawn in the sand, and there seems to be little room or tolerance for civil discourse between the sides. Arguments have risen and friendships collapsed over issues such as systemic racism, political ideologies, responses to global conflicts, and so on.

These may sound like topics specific to the political arena, but the church continuously finds herself caught up in these whirlwinds. It's likely that you know of a local church that has been forced to take a stand on some issue and encountered some measure of backlash and loss in the process. I've seen some leave a local church because a stance was too strong, while others left the same church because the stance wasn't strong enough!

While James doesn't provide answers to these specific debates, he certainly addresses how we are to posture ourselves, and pray, through challenges like these.

We will move through James chronologically, highlighting various essentials for effective prayer as they appear. Having said that, this is not a line-by-line study of the whole book. Because we aren't going to cover every verse, I recommend that you take a moment to read the focus text once or twice before diving into each new chapter, giving you a sense of the whole argument James is making as we unpack select verses.

I also encourage you to read James through this prayer lens, allowing his words to inform how you pray and live. It is transforming how we at NHOP pray, and I believe it will do the same for you.

But let it speak to you in other areas of your life as well. This epistle carries many parallels to the Sermon on the Mount, which deals so much with our character as the people of God. If the Holy Spirit is putting His finger on another area of your life as you read, then by all means put the book down, follow His lead, and respond to Him.

My prayer is that the church in Canada, and around the world, will walk in robes of white, reflecting the irresistible nature of Jesus as we pray *"Your kingdom come, your will be done"* (Matthew 6:10) in alignment with His heart. James is going to help us do that.

ESSENTIAL #1

An Eternal Mindset (James 1:2–18)

*Their loyalty is divided
between God and the world...*
(James 1:8, NLT)

Have you ever wondered why we pray? Or what prayer is? Prayer is often understood as asking for things and, yes, that is certainly part of it.

But here in the West, one could argue that, under that definition, there's not much need for prayer. We live in an age of excessive comfort, with an endless supply of entertainment through scores of media channels to keep us occupied through the day. We live under the blessing of the most advanced medical system in history, allowing us to live longer, healthier lives. We can connect with friends and family near and far like never before, and it seems like we're all just one viral video away from celebrity status and striking it rich.

We are the richest generation in the richest society in the history of mankind, and that makes life quite comfortable for most. Therefore, many believers in the West have a minimal, if not completely dormant, prayer life. We don't need anything. If prayer is about asking for things, why would we need to pray?

Prayer is about more than simply asking for things. It's the ongoing dialogue between a loving Creator and His beloved creation. It's the relational connection point between God and man. It's how we abide in the Vine (John 15). And as with any other relationship, this one must be nurtured with investments of time and energy. Prayer is where that happens.

In the Old Testament, God revealed Himself and His dealings with mankind specifically through His relationship with the people of Israel. Over the course of that relationship, a pattern clearly emerged. It began when God delivered Israel from Egypt in the Exodus, then declared them to be His own special treasure, set apart from the other nations of the earth (Exodus 19:5–6). When the Israelites saw God's mighty hand and outstretched arm give them the Promised Land in Joshua's generation, they walked with the Lord, generally speaking.

But they soon got comfortable in the covenantal blessings that obedience had brought them.

When Joshua died, Israel's heart began to wander. The next generation hadn't seen the works of the Lord firsthand. They hadn't been present when He caused the Jordan River to stand in a heap so they could cross over on dry land. They began to participate in the more carnally appealing worship practices of their neighbours, who worshiped Baal.

The tables soon turned and the people of Israel found themselves in servitude to the very people groups they had wandered after.

Here we see the pattern take shape. Israel cried out in anguish over their difficult circumstances, they repented, and then the Lord delivered. Israel thereafter walked in obedience for a season, got comfortable in the covenantal blessings they experienced, wandered from the Lord as they got too comfortable, and finally experienced the covenantal curses, the fruit of their sin, as they strayed. In the ensuing anguish, Israel would cry out again in prayer, causing the cycle to repeat.

This cycle repeats itself seven times in the book of Judges alone.

These stories have been preserved for us for a purpose: that we might learn from them and avoid making the same mistakes (1 Corinthians 10:6). Paul told the Corinthians that their hearts were as prone to wander as those of the Israelites and that they would be wise to heed the warnings provided by these stories.

We are no different from those generations of old. When we're aware of our spiritual poverty, we tend to lean into God more diligently. When times are good, we easily buy the deception that we don't need Him as much. This produces a wandering that leads us to a place of emptiness… and the cycle repeats.

ESSENTIAL #1: AN ETERNAL MINDSET

If we're honest, we could say that the Western church in general is on the downswing of that cycle. We have lived for generations in a time of prosperity, influence, and peace within our borders, so complacency comes to us naturally. One of the dangers of complacency is that it causes us to set our minds on temporal things, such as money and all it can buy, promotion, recognition, the praise of man, etc. While these things aren't evil in and of themselves, when our hearts fixate on them we slowly drown out the voice that reminds us we were made for eternity (Ecclesiastes 3:11, Revelation 22:1–4).

James wrote his letter to the church of the first century, which was largely comprised of Messianic Jews. There are several differences between the audience then and now. Quality of life is one. Most estimates suggest that the average life expectancy of that era, with their primitive medicinal practices, was approximately thirty to forty years. The comforts of technology and luxury were nothing like we have today.

Perhaps one of the most overlooked but glaring differences is that these people lived under Roman rule. They didn't have the rights, privileges, freedoms, or protections we have in Western democracies today.

Despite recent cultural and legislative trends, we still have it much better than the first-century believers did. Not only were those believers less than citizens, but many were considered enemies of the state. The emperors were worshiped as deities, and those who refused to worship them often did so at the expense of their lives.

These are some of the realities that shaped the context in which James wrote.

His letter to these believers opens with an encouragement to embrace the difficulties they were facing:

> Count it all joy, my brothers, when you meet trials of various kinds, for you know that the testing of your faith produces steadfastness. And let steadfastness have its full effect, that you may be perfect and complete, lacking in nothing. (James 1:2–4)

This is an encouragement to remain steadfast, persevere, or endure in the face of many trials and difficulties.

It can be hard for us to grasp the weight of this encouragement because we just don't have a frame of reference for the scope of persecution they experienced. In the West, the most common persecution we endure might be getting teased or ridiculed by peers. In some cases, this may cost us friendships, family relationships, careers, or businesses. This does hurt.

However, our freedoms of religion, conscience, and speech are, as of today, still protected by law. We don't gather to worship under fear of imprisonment or death.

If we observe the trends of our culture, though, we can see that these freedoms aren't necessarily guaranteed for life. While we may not face the same pressures today, we would be wise to heed James' call to steadfastness now, rather than wait for that pressure to increase.

THE WISDOM OF LIVING IN VIEW OF ETERNITY

In the following verses, James introduces two themes that appear several times in his letter: wisdom and prayer.

> If any of you lacks wisdom, let him ask God, who gives generously to all without reproach, and it will be given him. (James 1:5)

It seems like an interesting step, going from steadfastness in the face of trials to wisdom. But this theme runs throughout Scripture: wisdom maintains an eternal perspective, while foolishness is fixated on what is temporal.

Paul drew this same connection when he wrote that we are joint heirs with Christ. What an amazing statement! But Paul added that if we want to partake in His glorification as joint heirs, *"we must also share his suffering"* (Romans 8:17, NLT). This ought to make us pause to count the cost.

Paul had already done the math for himself, and he proceeded to share his conclusion on the matter: *"For I consider that the sufferings of this present time are not worth comparing with the glory that is to be revealed to us"* (Romans 8:18). It's like he was saying, "Look, guys, I've counted the cost: I've considered the glory that will be revealed to us for all eternity in Christ, and I've thought about what would be gained to deny Christ and live comfortably today… and it's not even close. You can't even compare the two! Choose the eternal glory!"

If you read the New International Version, you'll notice that *"revealed to us"* is instead translated as *"revealed in us."* This glory isn't just something we'll see but something that we'll partake in.

For examples of people who lived with this eternal mindset, we can look to Hebrews 11, the chapter often referred to as presenting the Hall of Faith. It is a roster of Old Testament people who were, and still are, revered as heroes of our faith. The writer of Hebrews highlights that they all had something in common:

> All these people were still living by faith when they died. They did not receive the things promised; they only saw them and welcomed them from a distance, admitting that they were foreigners and strangers on earth. People who say such things show that they are looking for a country of their own. If they had been thinking of the country they had left, they would have had opportunity to return. *Instead, they were longing for a better country—a heavenly one.* (Hebrews 11:13–16, NIV, emphasis added)

What gave these men and women the heroic faith to endure struggles? It was the understanding that their primary citizenship was in the Kingdom of God. They knew there was a coming glory far greater than anything they could achieve or receive in this age, so they spent their life's energy in pursuit of that promise.

Moses is one of the key figures highlighted in this chapter, and his example is one that should speak to us today:

> By faith Moses, when he was grown up, refused to be called the son of Pharaoh's daughter, choosing rather to be mistreated with the people of God than to enjoy the fleeting pleasures of sin. *He considered the reproach of Christ greater wealth than the treasures of Egypt*, for he was looking to the reward. (Hebrews 11:24–26, emphasis added)

Do we consider the reproach of Christ to be the path to greater wealth than success in the here and now? Or is the illusion of a comfortable life today enough to lull us into complacency?

Near the end of his letter, James points to some of these same heroes as examples of endurance. He argues that the reason the prophets are so revered is that they endured through suffering. They didn't recant when their unpopular messages began to cost them their comforts, like personal safety. They stayed true to the word and call God had given them. We love their writings and messages today, but their contemporaries generally hated what they had to say. These messengers endured that scorn to the end and are honoured for it today.

James also highlights Job, who struggled mightily with God yet never succumbed to the advice of his wife to curse God and die. James says that God's purpose in Job's trial was to demonstrate His compassion and mercy, which He did by giving Job far more at the end than he had at the beginning (James 5:11).

The New Testament extols those who endure temporal discomfort and persecutions for the sake of a future reward.

This boils down to a question of rewards and treasures. In Matthew 6:19–24, Jesus says we can't have it both ways: we can either pursue treasure in this life or in the age to come. We can't pursue both. We can spend our lives in pursuit of material wealth, but He warns us that those treasures are subject to theft and decay. Even if we manage to preserve them, we can't take them with us when we die.

On the other hand, we can spend our lives in such a way that we lay up treasure in heaven, treasure that can't decay or be stolen and will remain with us for eternity. This is the classic dilemma: we can have one treat now, or five treats later.

Only these stakes are much higher. On the plus side, the exchange rate for the eternal rewards is far more generous than we can imagine (Matthew 10:42, Isaiah 61:2–3,7–8, 10, Daniel 12:3, 1 Corinthians 3:10–14, 4:5).

This idea of an eternal mindset explains James' thought process. It explains what he means when he says that the poor have something to boast about and the rich are at a disadvantage (James 1:9–11). The rich are easily seduced into believing they are successful because of their accumulation of wealth, but everything they rejoice in will fade away, leaving them with nothing of lasting value at the end. They think they're safe and secure, but their riches are an illusion (Proverbs 18:11).

The poor have an advantage: fewer trappings to keep them from entering the Kingdom of God (Matthew 5:3, 19:24).

A prime example of this is seen in the life of Esau, who sold his birthright to his brother Jacob for a bowl of stew (Genesis 25). Was Jacob deceptive and manipulative, seizing an opportunity to prey on his brother in a moment of weakness? Yeah, probably. But Esau judged the situation with foolishness. He considered the temporal comfort of a full belly to be more valuable than his inheritance, which would have impacted his family for generations to come.

Anyone reading this story today can see that it was a foolish decision. Do you want to know how God judged that situation? I think we see a clue in Malachi 1:2–3: *"Yet Jacob I have loved; but Esau I have hated…"* (NKJV)

A more difficult expression of this idea is found in Hebrews 10:32–38. The writer praises his readers for how they endured the forfeiture of temporal comforts for the sake of the gospel in their early days and encourages them to maintain their endurance. Then he gives them this double-edged sword of an encouragement: *"Yet a little while, and the coming one will come and will not delay; but my righteous one shall live by faith, and if he shrinks back, my soul has no pleasure in him"* (Hebrews 10:37–38). A hard statement, yes, but he also inserts a rod of iron into their backbones with this encouragement: *"But we are not of those who shrink back…"* (Hebrews 10:39)

Beloved, if we are truly born of the Spirit (Ephesians 1:13–14), we will not be one of those who shrink back. The cost of taking up our cross to follow Him can't be compared to the glory that will be revealed in us! James agrees with this point: *"Blessed is the man who remains steadfast under trial, for when he has stood the test he will receive the crown of life, which God has promised to those who love him"* (James 1:12).

DOUBLE-MINDEDNESS AND DOUBT

Let's move on to James 1:6. Here we come to James' first comment on prayer, where he encourages the believers to pray for wisdom:

> But let him ask in faith, with no doubting, for the one who doubts is like a wave of the sea that is driven and tossed by the wind. *For that person must not suppose that he will receive anything from the Lord;* he is a *double-minded* man, unstable in all his ways. (James 1:6–8, emphasis added)

To ask with doubt is to be double-minded. Catch what James is saying: we should expect God *not* to answer when we ask in that doubting state! He continues this line of thinking again in the fourth chapter, where he addresses ineffective prayer:

> You ask and do not receive, because you ask wrongly, to spend it on your passions. You adulterous people! Do you not know that *friendship with the world is enmity with God?* Therefore whoever wishes to be a friend of the world makes himself an enemy of God… Cleanse your hands, you sinners, and purify your hearts, you *double-minded*. (James 4:3–4, 8, emphasis added)

Note the connection between the two passages: double-mindedness is linked to ineffective prayer. In the first passage, doubt is linked to double-mindedness. In the second passage, friendship with the world (temporal comfort) is the cause.

The New Living Translation picks up on this correlation and brings the second double-mindedness into the first passage: *"Such people should not expect to receive anything from the Lord. Their loyalty is divided between God and the world, and they are unstable in everything they do"* (James 1:7–8, NLT, emphasis added)

There's an underlying question in the opening of James' letter that we must answer. How we answer it will lay the foundation for either an effective or ineffective prayer life. That question is simple: where is my reward?

If our preferred reward is to live comfortably for these seventy or eighty years, we should expect to have a very hit-and-miss prayer life. If we pray with an eye toward those things that make life easier, James tells us that we won't receive what we ask for. Remember, he refers to that as asking amiss.

This is consistent with Jesus' teachings on prayer from the Sermon on the Mount (Matthew 6:25–34). Interestingly, He spends the first portion of that instruction also talking about temporal, though very necessary, things: food, drink, and clothing (Matthew 6:25). He implores His listeners not to be consumed with those things or grow anxious about them, pursuing them like the Gentiles do.

> *But seek first the kingdom of God and his righteousness, and all these things will be added to you.* (Matthew 6:33, emphasis added)

The primary value that ought to inform and drive our prayer is the Kingdom of God and His righteousness: *"Your kingdom come, your will be done, on earth as it is in heaven"* (Matthew 6:10). Not those things that we perceive will make our lives easier.

This should cause us to periodically pause and reflect on what motivates us in prayer.

At NHOP, one of our prioritized prayer focuses is government and the political sphere. We've had to ask ourselves this same question: what is our motive in praying for Christians to rise to positions of influence in government? Is it because we want to see justice and righteousness expressed in our land? Or is it because we want a government that thinks as we do and will support legislation that preserves our values and way of life?

Do you see the difference?

This is admittedly a difficult question to grapple with. We want to see the life-giving values of the Kingdom find expression in Canada, but we must remember that His ways are not ours, and His thoughts are higher than ours (Isaiah 55:8–9). Thus, the journey toward that destination often doesn't look the way we think it should in His good and perfect leadership.

ONE THING IS NEEDED

An effective prayer life is marked by a desire to see the Kingdom of God expressed on the earth however *He* sees fit. If that isn't truly our desire, how do we change so that it becomes our desire? An interesting phrase pops up three times in Scripture, "one thing," which I think holds the key to this shift.

The first mention of it comes to us from the life of King David, the man famously described by God as being after His own heart (1 Samuel 13:14). David used the phrase in this way:

> *One thing have I asked* of the Lord, *that will I seek after:* that I may dwell in the house of the Lord all the days of my life, to gaze upon the beauty of the Lord and to inquire in his temple. (Psalm 27:4, emphasis added)

David's one thing was a desire to be in the presence of the Lord, to gaze on His beauty and inquire of Him in that place.

The second mention is found in Luke, when Jesus visited the home of Martha and Mary. You likely know the story well: Martha was busy being a good host while Mary sat at the feet of Jesus and listened to His every word. Martha, annoyed about doing all the work alone, asked Jesus to take her side and make Mary help her. Martha was undoubtedly surprised by Jesus' answer: *"Martha, Martha, you are anxious and troubled about many things, but one thing is necessary. Mary has chosen the good portion, which will not be taken away from her"* (Luke 10:41–42, emphasis added)

To Jesus, Martha's well-intentioned service as a good host was second to the necessity of tuning in to His words with undivided focus. Mary figured out the one thing that was necessary, and Jesus wouldn't dissuade her from pursuing it.

The final reference is found in the third chapter of Paul's letter to the Philippians. He recounted how he had suffered the loss of all things for the sake of knowing Him, growing in the knowledge of Him. After acknowledging that he had not yet attained his goal, he made this statement: *"But one thing I do: forgetting what lies behind and straining forward to what lies ahead, I press on toward the goal for the prize of the upward call of God in Christ Jesus"* (Philippians 3:13–14, emphasis added)

Paul was focused on pressing forward every day of his life. He was never satisfied with yesterday's manna but had an insatiable desire to grow in the knowledge of Jesus. He repented and moved forward from the shortcomings and failures of the day before, simultaneously refusing to rest in his prior accomplishments.

If anybody could have rested on their laurels in ministry, it was him! Paul insisted that running hard isn't just for the young when he said, *"Let those of us who are mature think this way…"* (Philippians 3:15) This single-minded, wholehearted pursuit is the recommended heart posture for every believer, regardless of age or tenure in the Kingdom.

One thing we must seek, need, and do: we press on to know Him by drawing near, listening attentively to His voice by the indwelling Spirit, gazing on His beauty.[1] As we invest time and energy into this pursuit, we'll find ourselves desiring Him more than the trappings of this world.

THE PURITY OF SINGLE-MINDEDNESS

In addressing the double-mindedness of having one's loyalty divided between God and the world, James alludes to Psalm 24 when he says,

---

[1] We'll delve into this further in the next chapter.

"Cleanse your hands, you sinners, and purify your hearts, you double-minded" (James 4:8).

Psalms 24 and 15 deal with two questions: who can ascend the hill of the Lord, and who can stand in His holy place? These questions address how we approach God's presence, coming to Him in worship and/or prayer. Both psalms describe righteousness in the believer, summing it up by saying, *"He who has clean hands and a pure heart…"* (Psalm 24:4) In other words, the ones who draw near are the ones whose outward actions and inward motivations are clean and pure.

Most dictionaries are unanimous in their primary definition of the word pure. Something is pure when it's uncontaminated by a foreign substance. To be pure is to be free from mixture.

To have a pure heart is to have a heart set on one thing or person. A pure heart is a heart undivided in loyalty between God and the world; its love for God is uncontaminated with a love of mammon. It is set on giving all its attention and affection to Him.

James is telling us that the heart of a person with one eye on God and the other on the world is not pure; it is mixed, double-minded, and therefore will produce ineffective prayer.

If that describes us, what is the prescribed response? To wash our hands of evil deeds and to fix our hearts on one thing. These are both acts of repentance.

The first question we draw from James concerning prayer is simple: where is our primary reward? Are we coming to God half-heartedly, praying with one eye on the things we think will lead to our comfort? Or is our sole desire that His name be glorified and famous? Do we long for His Kingdom to find expression in our country, province, town, and life, at any cost? As long as we have divided desires on this matter, we are double-minded.

No combination of strategies, works, or polished prayers can get us around this one. God, who sees through all the externals, is looking for those whose hearts are loyal to Him, because He wants to show Himself strong on their behalf (2 Chronicles 16:9). Setting one's heart to love Him more than the comforts of this transient life is the first essential to praying effectively.

ESSENTIAL #2

A Listening Heart in Prayer (James 1:19–26)

You must all be quick to listen,
slow to speak...
(James 1:19, NLT)

Most of us probably remember the sound of our mother's voice saying, "God gave you two ears and one mouth, so listen twice as much as you speak!" Well, guess what? James agrees with mom.

> Know this, my beloved brothers: let every person be quick to hear, slow to speak... (James 1:19)

Mama was right. Something in our nature (pride) thinks we need to keep talking, that others need to hear what we have to say. Sometimes that's true.

But James tells us we need to have a posture that puts a greater emphasis on listening than speaking.

Whether conversing with peers, superiors, or those we oversee, it is wise to listen. When we listen, we gain information, which serves to inform our speech. When we speak without listening, we speak out of assumption... and I think we all know what happens when we assume. It is wise to listen and gather as much information as possible before speaking.

The book of Proverbs is loaded with thoughts on the wisdom of listening.[2]

While primarily addressing interpersonal relationships, this passage can certainly apply to our prayer lives as well. Of every relationship we have, shouldn't our relationship with Him be the one where we are most

---

[2] For a few examples, see Proverbs 1:5, 13:11, 18:13, 19:27, 21:28, and 28:9.

keen to start with listening? Who among us could possibly improve on anything He would have to say?

Let's consider an example from the life of Job. First, hear the Bible's description of him: *"There was a man in the land of Uz whose name was Job, and that man was blameless and upright, one who feared God and turned away from evil"* (Job 1:1). Sounds like a pretty good endorsement!

And yet when God came on the scene, His first statement to Job out of the whirlwind was this: *"Who is this that darkens counsel by words without knowledge?"* (Job 38:2) God made it perfectly clear that blameless and upright Job had nothing to bring to the table before God, in terms of wisdom or knowledge. God wasn't being angry or mean; He was being honest.

If blameless and upright Job darkened counsel with his words, maybe we would be smart to listen before speaking when we approach Him in prayer.

THE IMPORTANCE OF LISTENING

Let's start by defining what listening is, and what it isn't. Listening is not the same as hearing. Hearing is passive whereas listening is active. Oxford Learner's Dictionary describes hearing as being "aware of sounds with your ears."[3] It describes the process of auditory stimuli being picked up by our ears.

But listening involves *processing* those sounds, thinking through what they mean, and considering the associated applications or consequences. To listen is to "pay attention to somebody/something or something that you can hear."[4] Parents of growing children see this difference in their homes every day. Kids hear most of what their parents say, but that doesn't guarantee that they're listening. That part usually requires some training, development, and encouragement.

James similarly encourages his readers not to settle for just hearing the Word, but to focus on actually doing what it says (James 1:22). He

---

[3] "Hear," *Oxford Learner's Dictionaries*. Date of access: July 9, 2024 (https://www.oxfordlearnersdictionaries.com/definition/english/hear).

[4] "Listen," *Oxford Learner's Dictionaries*. Date of access: July 9, 2024 (https://www.oxfordlearnersdictionaries.com/definition/english/listen).

goes on to say that it is in the doing of what we hear that we are blessed (James 1:25). It's not enough to read the Bible or hear good messages; we must listen and respond to the Word to taste of its benefits. This requires more than speed reading on our part. We must take the Word in, meditate on it, and walk it out.

LISTENING IN THE BEGINNING

To see the importance of listening, we can go right to the beginning of the story in the Garden of Eden. God had created the whole of the physical realm by the word of His mouth, culminating in the creation of mankind.

He gave Adam and Eve paradise for a home, where they experienced unhindered relationship with God. Among all the blessings of life in a literal paradise, He gave them just one restriction: to forsake the fruit of the tree of the knowledge of good and evil (Genesis 2:17). He gave them free will as well, and to activate that will He gave them a choice.

We don't really know how long they lived in this paradise situation before succumbing to temptation, but they certainly lived in it longer than any of us have.

In Genesis 3, the serpent came to test Eve. His temptation was rooted in a question over what God had said. Genesis 2:17 clearly says that God had told Adam they could eat of any tree in the garden, but they were not to eat of the fruit from that one tree. The serpent's question to Eve tested her ability to listen: *"Did God actually say, 'You shall not eat of <u>any</u> tree in the garden'?"* (Genesis 3:1, emphasis added)

Note the twisting of God's words. The serpent made God's boundary sound much more restrictive than it actually was. Eve valiantly tried to reply with what the Lord had said, but she was just a little off: *"We may eat of the fruit of the trees in the garden, but God said, 'You shall not eat of the fruit of the tree that is in the midst of the garden, <u>neither shall you touch it</u>, lest you die"* (Genesis 3:2–3, emphasis added). She did well to refute the accusation, but she still made God's boundary overly restrictive, though I suppose it would be wise not to touch the fruit that could kill you.

Seeing that his target was a little off-balance, the serpent went all-in, calling God's statement an outright lie (Genesis 3:4).

Somewhere down the line in those earliest days, Adam and Eve had trouble listening to what God said. God had apparently given Adam clear instructions concerning trees and fruit before He created Eve. Did Adam miscommunicate God's instructions to Eve? Or did he communicate it clearly, but Eve didn't pay attention as closely as she should have? We don't know. But we do know that they both bought the serpent's lie that God was bluffing concerning the fruit of that tree. And the rest is history.

Satan is a liar, deceiver, and accuser (Zechariah 3:1, John 8:44, Genesis 3:13, 2 Corinthians 11:3, Revelation 12:9–10, 20:10). His primary activities toward us include undermining and twisting all that God has said. He's a bit like a one-trick pony in that way. It's even how he tempted Jesus in the wilderness (Matthew 4:1–11).

Maintaining a close walk with God begins with not only hearing Him, through His written Word and the indwelling Spirit, but listening to Him and doing what He prescribes. Jesus told us that this is how He lived and ministered; He only did what He saw the Father doing and said what the Father told Him to say (John 5:19, 12:49–50). Jesus didn't live by bread alone but testified that His sustenance came from listening to every word that came from the mouth of God and doing the will of His Father (Matthew 4:4, John 4:34).

If Jesus' ministry depended on listening to God, how much more should it be a central practice in our lives today?

It is interesting to note the role of listening in the *shema* of Deuteronomy 6:4–5, which is "the great call to worship and identity of Israel as God's people."[5] This is the passage Jesus quoted when a lawyer tried to stump Him by asking, "Which is the greatest commandment?"

> Hear, O Israel: The Lord our God, the Lord is one. You shall love the Lord your God with all your heart and

---

[5] William D. Mounce, *Mounce's Complete Expository Dictionary of Old and New Testament Words* (Grand Rapids, MI: Zondervan, 2006), 326.

with all your soul and with all your might. (Deuteronomy 6:4–5)

This great characterization of God and His people's relationship to Him begins with the *shema* command. The word is translated as "hear," but its definition goes further. *Shema* means "to hear, listen, pay attention to, perceive, obey, proclaim, announce."[6]

Yes, its meaning extends far beyond a passive hearing. The *shema* was a call to pay attention to the declaration of the supremacy and oneness of God, to perceive it by living in conscious awareness of it, to obey the call to love Him wholeheartedly, and to proclaim and announce to others this same truth and call. It is an Old Testament equivalent of the New Testament call to respond to the gospel and call others to respond to the gospel… and it all starts with listening.

TWO POSTURES OF LISTENING

There are two primary postures from which we listen, and it is important that we learn to carry them both. These postures can seem like opposites at first glance, but upon closer look we see that they complement and strengthen one another. This is consistent with how we grapple with many of the attributes of God. He is equally the God of mercy *and* the just Judge, for example. In a similar way, these two postures are an expression of our response to the vast revelations of the majesty and mercy of God in our prayer lives.

We first listen from a posture of humility. It is wise for us to pray with an awareness of which one in the conversation is God Almighty, and which is mortal man. We all wrestle with pride, and it's easy for us to think we're bigger than we are.

This isn't only true of the overly confident ones among us; pride also lurks in the shadows when we overemphasize our weaknesses. We can be deceived into thinking that our sin is too great for Christ's blood to cover, or our weakness too inept for God's grace to work with. Is that not also pride, making our sin greater than His grace? It's important that

---

[6] Ibid., 325.

we maintain an accurate estimation of ourselves: we're not as great as we think we are, nor are we too far gone for Him to reach us.

When considering the gap between our capacity for pride and the need for us to come in silent humility, Solomon has some wisdom for us. His reign constitutes the glory days of Israel's history. They enjoyed their greatest prosperity and peace under his administration, as God made Solomon greater in wisdom than any other on earth. Kings and people from surrounding nations came to see for themselves whether the rumours of this man's wisdom were true (1 Kings 4:20–34).

Pride surely came easily for Solomon. Yet in all his wisdom and experimentation, he concluded that humility is the proper posture with which to approach the God of heaven and earth:

> As you enter the house of God, keep your ears open and your mouth shut. It is evil to make mindless offerings to God. Don't make rash promises, and don't be hasty in bringing matters before God. After all, God is in heaven, and you are here on earth. *So let your words be few.* (Ecclesiastes 5:1–2, NLT, emphasis added)

Even in all his wisdom, Solomon concluded that it was wise to come before the Lord in silence first. It's easy for us to lean on our own understanding, falling into the assumption that we know what God is thinking, or what He would do in certain situations. This leads to presumption in our prayer lives, and presumption isn't something we want to bring before the Lord (1 Samuel 15:23, Psalm 19:13). We should keep Isaiah 55:9 close to heart: *"For as the heavens are higher than the earth, so are my ways higher than your ways and my thoughts higher than your thoughts."* When we remember that His thoughts are higher than our own, we remember to come to Him in a posture of listening.

It's easy to adopt a posture of listening when we don't know what to do. The tricky part is in maintaining that posture when we're confident that we *do* know what to do.

Israel ran into that problem while moving into the Promised Land in Joshua 9. After a couple of big victories, undoubtedly feeling good about themselves, they failed to seek God's counsel when the local Gibeonites came asking for peace, posing as foreigners from a faraway land. Joshua and the elders made a covenant of peace with them when they should have driven them out of the land like the other inhabitants.

God miraculously used that covenant to help Israel defeat five other Canaanite nations, but that covenant also came back to cost Israel hundreds of years later during the reigns of Saul and David (2 Samuel 21). At the end of the day, it was a mistake they shouldn't have made, and they made it because they neglected to listen to God out of their own self-confidence.

I think we see a modern-day example of this play out in every election cycle. It's a reality in Canada, but it's especially clear in the United States, where voters have just two parties to choose from. Each cycle, we hear leaders from the body of Christ boldly declare that it is the will of God for Christians to vote for one party, and other leaders declare with equal boldness that it's His will for the other party to win. Both sides make clear and compelling arguments from Scripture to confirm their stance. What do we do with that?

The point is not for us to try to figure out who is in presumption and who isn't. That's a pointless pursuit. He alone knows our hearts and minds, and therefore only He can answer that question rightly (1 Corinthians 4:4–6). My point is that people speak out of presumption from both sides of the debate, because both sides assume God agrees with them: "We have the right theology." When both sides jump to making bold, presumptuous statements, it only serves to muddy the waters. A little more listening and a little less talking might be helpful.

The point of raising this open-ended question can be seen in another story from the life of Joshua, this time from Joshua 5. He had just led the first generation of freeborn Israelites across the Jordan River, set foot on the Promised Land, and camped outside Jericho. They observed the Passover and re-established their covenant with God by circumcising all the males. They were fed by manna for the last time, a sign that they were going to live on the crops of the land from that day forward.

On the eve of their offensive, Joshua received a visitor:

> When Joshua was by Jericho, he lifted up his eyes and looked, and behold, a man was standing before him with his drawn sword in his hand. And Joshua went to him and said to him, *"Are you for us, or for our adversaries?"* And he said, *"No;* but I am the commander of the army of the Lord. Now I have come… Take off your sandals from your feet, for the place where you are standing is holy." (Joshua 5:13–15, emphasis added)

It's both funny and alarming that Joshua didn't even have the right question, let alone the right answer! We so easily think in terms of us versus them. We only see two or three possible answers, but He sees things very differently. He sits enthroned above the earth and sees everything in His omniscience, while we only see what's right in front of us.

Joshua could only understand the Angel of the Lord being *for* them or *against* them. But the answer he got was "No. Neither." The proper posture was not to give the Angel of the Lord an ultimatum, but rather for Joshua to get in line and make sure he was on the Lord's side. God gets to draw the lines, not us. Humility is how we stay in line with Him.

I know that we aren't always to be completely silent. Prayer does involve us bringing forward petitions, supplications, and requests (Daniel 6:11, Matthew 6:9–13, Ephesians 6:18, Philippians 4:6, 1 Timothy 2:1, 5:5, 1 John 5:15). But when we engage in prayer from a place of presumption, speaking before listening, it can come out like a list of demands. A humble posture involves us taking a different approach. I've heard Rob Parker, founder of NHOP, say it this way: "We don't tell God, we ask Him."

He is God. We are not. He is eternal, omniscient, and wise. We are finite, limited in knowledge, and lacking in wisdom. In fact, any wisdom we do have is linked directly to the measure of the fear of the Lord we walk in (Proverbs 1:7). No information, intelligence, or solution we bring to Him will improve on what He has in mind. We do well to come to Him in humility, listen for His leading, then add our voice in agreement as we pray.

ESSENTIAL #2: A LISTENING HEART *in* PRAYER

One way to do this is to pray the Word of God itself. When we pray passages of Scripture, such as the apostolic prayers in the New Testament, we are praying that which has already been inspired by the Holy Spirit (2 Timothy 3:16). When we pray the inspired Word of God, according to the same intent with which it was written, we can be confident that we are praying in agreement with His heart and His will, confident because we are following His lead. That's the whole point: in prayer, we ought to listen before we speak from a posture that acknowledges that He is God, we are not, and things will go much better if He takes the lead instead of us.

The second posture of listening we embrace is one of devotion. We see this posture in two of the "one thing" examples introduced in the first chapter.

Let's first consider the example of Mary from Luke 10. Her posture of sitting at Jesus' feet and listening was clearly motivated by devotion, a love for Jesus and what He had to say. To Martha, it probably looked more like laziness. But to Mary, being near Jesus and hearing what He had to say was too good an opportunity to miss.

It seems likely that she did this at a cost. Knowing her sister as well as she would have, Mary likely knew that her choice to sit and listen would create relational tension with Martha. Taking her place among the disciples also would have been a cultural no-no. This is not a posture she stumbled into, but a deliberate choice she made to draw near and sit at His feet. She was willing to pay a price to express her love and devotion.

The most important point of this account isn't the fact that Mary sat at His feet, but that she listened to every word Jesus spoke. It's great that Mary was close to Jesus, but that doesn't guarantee she was paying attention to Him. The first commandment says that we are to love Him with all our minds, and that's the key activity Mary was engaged in.

Distraction is one of the greatest challenges for us in the twenty-first century. It's a challenge because it's not always bad, but it keeps us from reaching for what's best. Our society seems to move at a pace we weren't created to sustain. Twenty-four-hour news cycles, the global conversation forum of social media, and the constant stimulation of televisions, smartphones, and tablets have conditioned us to mentally jump from one thing to the next. Between work and extracurriculars, our lives get busier and busier.

We can look at the early church for our example. They daily connected with one another in the temple and each other's homes (Acts 2:46). That's almost unheard of today. When it comes to our walk with the Lord, we're losing the art of what A.W. Tozer, C.S. Lewis, and others have called long and loving meditation. How many of us can honestly say that we can remain in silence and solitude for five minutes or longer without fidgeting? When we make time to be in the Word and prayer, do we keep our phones handy, just in case someone needs to reach us?

It's not enough for us to simply make room for quiet time, only to be distracted by our nearby phone or thoughts of everything we have to do today or the TV we left on in the background. That would be like Mary sitting at Jesus' feet while playing with her hair, twiddling her thumbs, and perhaps paying more attention to one of the disciples sitting nearby. The one thing needed was to give Jesus her *attention*.

The same one thing is needed today.

Consider this a heads up to the seriousness of the challenge we face. It's an opportunity for a modern-day application of James' warnings to the rich. All these distractions seek to draw our eyes and hearts away from the One who really matters, luring us to invest in the wrong treasure. It's important for us to be resolute and steadfast in self-control, making space in our schedules, hearts, and minds for Him alone. We must train ourselves to slow down, be quiet, and listen.

More than ever, we need to be able to confess, with David, *"I have calmed and quieted my soul, like a weaned child with its mother; like a weaned child is my soul within me"* (Psalm 131:2). A nursing infant is often anxious and tense when it first comes to its mother, and then they can often be distracted while feeding. But a weaned child comes to its mother by choice, and their coming is more an expression of wanting companionship than of frantically seeking a need to be met. Let's seek to be children of God who don't only come to Him in times of need and panic but who choose and delight to be with Him.

ESSENTIAL #2: A LISTENING HEART *in* PRAYER

Speaking of David, Psalm 27 is the other "one thing" we should look at. The one thing David desired was to dwell in the house of the Lord, to gaze upon His beauty and inquire in His temple (Psalm 27:4). Note that this is what he desired. This wasn't a hobby or something he did out of religious duty; it's what he wanted most in life.

For a little bit of context, let's consider what "the house of the Lord" meant to David. When he finally became king over Israel, he set out immediately to accomplish two things. The first was to conquer Jerusalem, a city of eternal significance in the heart and plan of God (2 Samuel 5:1–10). Though in the heart of the Promised Land, the city was still occupied by the Jebusites, as the Israelites had for centuries failed to drive them out. This city had been home to Melchizedek and was the site of Mount Moriah, where Abraham encountered God when he had been willing to lay down Isaac centuries before. David knew something was up with this city, and he needed to claim it.

The next thing he did was bring the Ark of the Covenant into his new capital. Since its capture by the Philistines and subsequent return, the Ark had remained in relative obscurity. This is significant. From the days of the Exodus and Israel's wilderness wanderings, the Ark's resting place had been in the heart of the Tabernacle of Moses, in the heart of the encampment of the entire nation. More than just a piece of furniture, the Ark of the Covenant was where Israel understood God's manifest presence to dwell on the earth. He was enthroned on the cherubim, and He Himself had said He would meet with them above the mercy seat, between the cherubim (2 Samuel 6:2, Exodus 25:22). This was the resting place of the presence of God!

The Tabernacle of Moses had rested in Shiloh since Israel settled in Canaan, but after its capture the Ark never returned there during Saul's reign. David sought to correct that by bringing the Ark back into the heart of the nation, literally and figuratively.

But instead of sending it back to the Tabernacle of Moses, David pitched a tent in Jerusalem near his palace and set the Ark there. He wanted to be near the presence of God. Then he funded 288 singers and four thousand musicians to worship night and day before the Ark as their full-time occupation. Think of the millions that would cost today!

Could you imagine a federal government funding night and day worship and prayer?

Here's the point. David set the Ark of the Covenant, the resting place of the presence of God, in a tent in the city of Jerusalem and then paid Levites to sing to it. They weren't singing to the box but ministering to the Lord, who sat enthroned on the box. Whether or not the Ark was concealed, we don't know. But from the sounds of Psalm 27:4, David loved going out to this Tabernacle, the house of the Lord, and gazing on the beauty of the Lord. Did he see the glory of God? I don't know for sure, but it seems like he did. Either way, we can be confident that he drew near to the presence of God and gazed.

In the New Covenant, gazing looks a little different. Sometimes God's manifest presence does show up amidst His people, and they see something of His glory.

But there is another way we can gaze on Him in our day-to-day lives. In Ephesians 1, Paul shares with the believers of Ephesus one of the prayers he often prayed for them:

> I do not cease to give thanks for you, remembering you in my prayers, that the God of our Lord Jesus Christ, the Father of glory, may give you the Spirit of wisdom and of revelation in the knowledge of him, having *the eyes of your hearts* enlightened... (Ephesians 1:16–18, emphasis added)

Paul prayed that the eyes of our hearts would be enlightened to see Him, that we would be able to gaze on Him. In the New King James Version, the word "understanding" is used in place of "heart."

How do we gaze on Him with the eyes of our heart, or understanding? We read the Bible. But we don't just read it, we meditate on it.

John referred to Jesus as *"the Word [made] flesh"* (John 1:14). Those who lived and walked with Jesus were watching the exact representation of the Father in action (Hebrews 1:3). Jesus even went so far as to tell Philip, *"Whoever has seen me has seen the Father"* (John 14:9). That would have been amazing for them, but what about us today?

Jesus also stated that the Scriptures bear witness to Him (John 5:39). In other words, they point to Him! They unveil who He is and what He is like.

The two disciples on the road to Emmaus got a master class in this truth when the risen Jesus Himself unpacked all the Scriptures from Moses to the prophets, explaining how they all pointed to Him (Luke 24:13–35). If there was ever a Bible study that felt like drinking from a fire hydrant, that was probably it!

The point is this: the Bible points to Jesus, the Word of God made flesh. There's a Man in those pages, and He is waiting to be encountered by those who will search for Him. But we don't find Him by skimming through or reading quickly. Jesus declared Himself to be a Bridegroom (John 3:29, Matthew 22:2, 25:1–6, Revelation 19:6–9) and that shows through in the Word. It's not so much a textbook to be dissected critically as it is a love letter, an unveiling of His heart and thoughts toward us, His betrothed. It is important that we study the Word. But when we limit our study to an academic or mental exercise, we miss the point.

The scribes and Pharisees had undertaken the academic task of searching the Scriptures incredibly well, but they completely missed the One those Scriptures pointed to (John 5:39). This is what Paul pointed out to the Corinthians in the beginning of his first letter, making clear that human wisdom and natural thinking cannot lead us to the knowledge of God. That can only be revealed to us through the Spirit as a gracious gift of illumination.

Have you ever received a love letter? Chances are you didn't plough through it quickly and put it away. You probably read it, reread it, and then spent time rehearsing portions of it in your mind throughout the following days and weeks. We similarly encounter Him in the Word by reading slowly and engaging in long and loving meditation.

When we think of meditation, we often conjure up images of eastern meditation practices: legs crossed, eyes closed, humming sounds, etc. But the Hebrew idea of meditation from the Old Testament is a bit different.

A few different Hebrew words are translated to refer to meditation, and some of their definitions may surprise you.

In Psalm 1, the blessed man is said to meditate (*hagah*). The definition of this Hebrew term includes words like growl, speak, utter, moan, lament, and mutter, alongside the idea of pondering something.[7]

In Psalm 19, when David prayed that the meditation (*hegyon*) of his heart would be pleasing to God, he used a word that carried the idea of muttering or thinking aloud, perhaps setting it to a melody.[8]

When we consider the Hebrew words that are translated as "meditate," we get the idea that meditation may not be a silent activity.

Consider this in the context of Moses' charge to Joshua during their transfer of power:

> This Book of the Law shall not depart from your *mouth*, but you shall *meditate [hagah] on it day and night*, so that you may be careful to do according to all that is written in it. For then you will make your way prosperous, and then you will have good success. (Joshua 1:8, emphasis added)

The definition applied to this usage of the word meditate is as follows: "meditate, ponder, give serious thought and consideration to selected information, with a possible implication of *speaking in low tones reviewing the material*."[9] Moses essentially told Joshua that the way to keep the Word close is to not only read it but keep repeating it to yourself throughout the day.

We gaze on Him by meditating on the Word. We find passages that speak of His nature and character, expressed by what He teaches, commands, and does, and study them. But we don't stop there: we keep reciting them. Better yet, we turn them into prayer. We don't lean on our own understanding in interpreting the Word; rather, we lean into the One who wrote the Word for His understanding.

Can you imagine what it would be like to read *The Lord of the Rings* along with J.R.R. Tolkien, or *The Chronicles of Narnia* along with C.S.

---

[7] James Swanson, *Swanson's Dictionary of Biblical Languages: Hebrew Old Testament, Second Edition* (Bellingham, WA: Logos Bible Software, 2001), #2047.
[8] Ibid., #2053.
[9] Ibid., emphasis added.

ESSENTIAL #2: A LISTENING HEART *in* PRAYER

Lewis? How much more insight would you glean by being able to stop after any given paragraph and ask, "What did you mean by that?" How much richer would the story become to you? How much more excited would you be to read it again, as the author gives you interpretive keys to unlock aspects of the story?

This is what is available to us with the Bible! The same Holy Spirit who inspired these authors to write the Bible dwells within us today. It's His job to search the deep things of God and make them known to us, and to take what is of Jesus and make it known to us (1 Corinthians 2:10–13, John 16:12–15). I would suggest that it's more than a job to Him. He really loves doing it, and He's quite good at it.

In the New Covenant we gaze on the beauty of God primarily by meditating lovingly and long on the Word of God, incorporating it into our dialogue with the Holy Spirit throughout the day. As we rehearse these passages in our minds, we listen to the Holy Spirit, allowing His leading to enlighten the eyes of our hearts. This is how we gaze in the New Covenant, and it is the primary way through which we set our hearts to listen from a posture of devotion.

LISTENING FROM BOTH POSTURES

So we listen from a posture of humility, remembering that He is God and we are not. We also listen from a posture of devotion, as an expression of our desire to be near Him, hear from Him, and grow in our experiential knowledge of Him. As mentioned at the beginning of this chapter, it's important to listen from both postures.

When we only listen from a posture of humility, we can get stuck in a rut. We can find ourselves thinking, "I'm a sinner saved by grace, a complete wretch… and I'll never be any more than that." On the other hand, when we only approach God as a friend we can become very familiar and cavalier toward Him, forgetting to approach Him with the honour He is due. This approach can lead to us bring God down to our level and pray in presumption.

Both postures are good and the ideas behind them are true, but neither are the whole truth on their own. We are sinners saved by grace who are deeply loved by God, betrothed to Christ, and seated with Him in heavenly places.

This is perfectly exemplified in some of Jesus' final words to His disciples before going to the cross:

> No longer do I call you servants, for the servant does not know what his master is doing; but I have called you friends, for all that I have heard from my Father I have made known to you. (John 15:15)

We love to focus on the phrase *"I have called you friends,"* but we should note that He first said *"No longer do I call you servants."* This means that the disciples started out as servants. They held the posture of a servant, and Jesus is the One who graduated them to friend status.

We often want to promote ourselves to a friend, leaving our servant status behind. But Jesus cautioned against that. In Luke 14:7–11, He suggested that we seek to occupy the lowest places and let the Master declare us worthy of greater honour. When we presume to take a position of greater honour for ourselves, we risk being humbled by that same Master.

Indeed, Jesus criticized the Pharisees for their love of seats of honour at banquets and feasts (Matthew 23:6). We know that God resists the proud and gives grace to the humble. So we need to ask ourselves: which treatment do we want to receive from Him?

When we only think of ourselves as friends before the Lord, we set ourselves up for offence. How? We can start to believe that God should only act in ways that benefit us or make us feel good. Bill Johnson said it very well when describing his heart response to the passing of his wife: "Is God my friend? Yeah, *but He was my Lord before He was my friend.* And my friendship with God can only go where His lordship has already been."[10]

Johnson made the point that God reserves the right to be God, that He doesn't owe us any explanations, and that He isn't required to lead us

---

[10] Bill Johnson, "Breaking the Bread of My Soul," *YouTube*. July 18, 2022 (https://www.youtube.com/watch?v=LbmKDFcG-vE&ab_channel=BillJohnsonTeaching%28Official%29). Quote begins at 7:04. Emphasis added.

only into what makes us feel good. He has already given us eternal life in exchange for our sin, and we are forever indebted to Him for that. He is first and foremost our Lord and Master. If we keep that posture, every subsequent invitation into friendship with Him is overwhelmingly kind. Perhaps more importantly, we won't be offended when we don't get exactly what we want.

Some worry that taking this posture of humility will keep us from experiencing the love and kindness we see on the friendship side of the ledger. The reality is that keeping this posture of humility magnifies the revelation of His grace and kindness! He has forgiven our sins, declared us righteous, and given us eternal life when we were guilty of sin and deserving of its punishment. He owes us nothing. And yet He insists on making us joint heirs with His Son and seating us with Him in heavenly places.

When we only understand ourselves as friends of God, we consider this treatment as something owed to us. But where is the joy in that? It's far more beneficial for us to live in a posture of humility, allowing these revelations to escort our hearts into places of awe, wonder, gratitude, thanksgiving, and worship. More than beneficial, the posture of humility is essential; as we'll explore later, God resists the proud but gives grace to the humble.

Jesus Himself combined these two revelations when He taught us to pray, *"Our Father in heaven, hallowed be your name"* (Matthew 6:9). There it is, perfectly succinct: friendship and humility, in prayer. This heart of gratitude and wonder also comes through in the Psalms:

> When I look at your heavens, the work of your fingers,
> the moon and the stars, which you have set in place,
> *what is man that you are mindful of him,* and the son
> of man that you care for him? (Psalm 8:3–4, emphasis
> added)

Daniel and the apostle John received these complementary revelations in a special way. Both knew by revelation that they were deeply loved by God (Daniel 10:11, 19, John 13:23, 19:26, 20:2, 21:7, 20), but both also had encounters where they knew without a shadow of a doubt that Jesus was on an entirely different level from them. This produced the fear of the Lord in them (Daniel 10:4–19, Revelation 1:17).

My prayer for myself and the church is that we would all live—and pray—from a healthy grasp of both the friendship and fear of the Lord.

POWER COMES FROM LISTENING

If you're reading this book, chances are that you hunger to have a powerful prayer life and see God move in your family, neighbourhood, church, and nation in response to your prayers. That's a good thing! Jesus publicly praised John the Baptist for aggressively advancing the Kingdom of God (Matthew 11:12), so it's safe to say that He approves of a heart that longs to be part of His Kingdom's advance.

But where does power to advance the Kingdom in prayer come from? There are many layers to this question. Relative to our topic, however, Scripture makes a convincing argument that powerful prayers come from a posture of listening.

The prophet Jeremiah lived in the southern kingdom of Judah in the generation leading up to its demise and exile to Babylon. His message, like most prophetic messages, was to call the people of Judah back to obedience and a right relationship with the Lord.

Jeremiah 23 shows us that one of the challenges he faced was crowded airwaves: many claimed to be prophets and publicly pronounced messages they knew would be palatable and pleasing to the people. A handful of prophets brought merciful warnings that people should turn in repentance so God would relent from the catastrophe on the horizon. This included prophets like Zephaniah or Joel.

But a multitude of prophets prophesied that everything was good. "Keep doing what you're doing," they essentially said. They prophesied promises of peace, safety, and prosperity to the ones who stubbornly followed their own desires over obedience to the Lord.

Note what God had to say about these self-proclaimed prophets:

> For who among them has stood in the council of the Lord to see and to hear his word, or who has paid attention to his word and listened?
>
> ...I did not send the prophets, yet they ran; I did not speak to them, yet they prophesied. *But if they had stood in my council, then they would have proclaimed my words to my people, and they would have turned them from their evil way,* and from the evil of their deeds...
>
> Is not my word like fire, declares the Lord, and like a hammer that breaks the rock in pieces? (Jeremiah 23:18, 21–22, 29, emphasis added)

Those who prophesied their own thoughts, dreams, and wishes did not bring words that produced fruit. Nobody turned. No lives were changed. Granted, that was kind of the point of their words.

But God's point here is that He is the One who knows the hearts and minds of all mankind, and He can bring a word that produces change. His word comes like a fire, or like a hammer that breaks the rock into pieces.

God asked Job if he could shout at the clouds to make them rain, or cause lightning to strike at his command (Job 38:34). The obvious answer is "No." But God can.

On the flip side, Jesus wowed His disciples when He did the opposite and shut down a storm with just a couple of words (Mark 4:39). All our most persuasive arguments, well-crafted sentences, and thoroughly researched points are nothing compared to the *rhema* Word of the Lord.

A trend has emerged in the prayer movement over the past few years, and it has to do with the practice of making decrees. There are several examples in Scripture of God's people being instructed to make statements or perform certain symbolic gestures to declare what the Lord was going to do. But we can sometimes lose focus of a key component of that process: those messengers acted in responsive obedience to what the Lord was already saying or doing.

When we start decreeing without listening, we can quickly find ourselves with ineffective prayer lives. When we skip the listening step, these decrees become little more than declarations of our wishes, with God's name attached to them in the hope that He'll be pressured to answer.

If you think about it, that's manipulation—and the One who is called faithful and true cannot be manipulated.

These man-initiated decrees typically go unanswered. Unanswered prayers or decrees can give rise to doubt, hope deferred, and eventually lead to many giving up on prayer because they tried it and it didn't work.

Decrees are great and powerful when initiated by the Lord. When we echo what the Lord is saying, the decree will burn like fire and smash stony places to pieces in the Spirit. That builds faith and advances the Kingdom. But if we throw a bunch of decrees at the wall and hope one sticks, it has a negative overall effect. Let's be people who seek to hit the mark with our prayers or decrees every time, by listening to what He is saying and agreeing with that.

If any prayers can confidently be decreed, they would be the prayers found in the Word. He's already inspired and preserved them for us. They're not our ideas, they're His. We just remember to stay in a posture of asking instead of telling, and when He speaks, we declare that. Don't let the pressure of having the freshest word or boldest decree draw you away from a posture of listening.

APPLYING BEFORE DECLARING

The last thing to point out about listening in prayer brings us back to the first chapter of James: *"receive with meekness the implanted word, which is able to save your souls. But be doers of the word, and not hearers only, deceiving yourselves"* (James 1:21–22). This ties back to the humility posture.

We often find it easier to apply the Word to others instead of ourselves. It's so easy to listen to a sermon and think, "I know exactly who needs to hear this." And we usually don't mean ourselves! Or we might have our eyes opened to a particular passage and think, "I can't wait to tell so-and-so. They would really benefit from this." But James instructed us to let the Word convict and correct us before we seek to apply it to someone else's situation.

When we embody the Word before sharing or praying it, it carries much greater weight. This is on par with Jesus' instructions to deal with the plank in our own eye before thinking about the speck in our brother's eye (Matthew 7:4), and to put into practice what we've heard, lest we lose the little bit we have received (Mark 4:24–25). This principle is also reflected by Paul when he emphasized self-control and personal discipline, lest he find himself personally disqualified though he had preached to others (1 Corinthians 9:27).

This is why James says that we are blessed in doing the Word, not just hearing it, and not just applying it to others. The Word is able to save our souls, not only those of everybody else.

The importance of listening is underscored by James: *"If you claim to be religious but don't control your tongue, you are fooling yourself, and your religion is worthless"* (James 1:26, NLT). The example Jesus set for us was one of meekness and humility, and of taking every cue from the Father. This is the example we are invited to follow.

We must learn to control our tongues, not just in what we say, but in when and how much. Let us be those who are quick to listen and slow to speak in our relationships with one another, but especially in our prayer lives before Him.

ESSENTIAL #3

Be Slow to Anger (James 1:19–20)

> *...for the anger of man does not produce the righteousness of God.*
> (James 1:20)

Before we move on to the second chapter of James, there's one more thing we need to look at from this passage. You may have noticed that in the last chapter we skipped over James' instruction to be slow to anger. That's because this bit of instruction gets its own chapter.

While this epistle is timeless and always applicable to our lives, I think this aspect of James' writing needs a little extra attention today.

The messages that grew to become this book originated in the days of the COVID-19 pandemic. It was a season of immense pressure for us in North America. Seeing that we've never known war on our shores, it was arguably the most trying season in a generation.

Fear, anxiety, loneliness, depression, and many other stressors took hold as the instructions to spend two weeks "to flatten the curve" turned into orders to isolate at home indefinitely. The rapid development of new vaccines to target the virus stirred a strong uneasiness in many, and as governments pushed to see a hundred percent of their populations inoculated, many resisted.

In Canada, this resistance climaxed in a convoy of truckers from across the land descending on Ottawa in protest of vaccine mandates. The Freedom Convoy became a real hot-button issue as it occupied downtown Ottawa for a full month. The arguments surrounding this protest reverberated across the country and divided many families, friendships, and churches.

The season clearly put a lot of pressure on people of all ages and genders, and Christians were not immune.

COVID-19 wasn't the only disruptive event of that season. George Floyd's tragic death in the spring of 2020 brought racial tensions to the forefront of our social consciousness in a way not seen in decades, spawning demonstrations across the U.S. and Canada. The mistreatment of Canada's Indigenous peoples at the hands of the church and federal government took centre stage once again, as unmarked graves were reportedly discovered on residential school properties. These events stirred up all sorts of debate on what responses or reparations are required, and how justice should be established and upheld. The various solutions and responses created more strain and division.

For the church, these pressures added to concerns that had been simmering for a few years. In 2015, a three-term Conservative government was ousted by Justin Trudeau and the Liberal Party. This upset much of the evangelical church, as many of them believe the Conservative party is more closely aligned with their values.

Prime Minister Trudeau and the new Liberal government quickly got to work, passing several bills that established and promoted their vision for Canada. Many of these bills were contrary to values held by many Christians. This bred an uneasiness in many believers, and it would be reasonable to speculate that this long-brewing anxiety fuelled many evangelicals' reactions and responses to the government's decisions during the COVID years. There was a lot of pent-up frustration.

While COVID continues to recede in the rear-view mirror, frustration still simmers. Plenty of new issues today are producing the same frustrations. Whether or not there's a catalytic crisis, we must acknowledge that there's hardly a time when someone *isn't* mad at the government.

Which brings us to the focus of this chapter: anger. The pressures of those few years caused frustration and anger to bubble up and spill into the public discourse. Granted, it could have been worse… but anger was there, nonetheless.

I'm pointing out anger specifically as it relates to frustrations with government, but this point extends into almost every area of our lives.

If we stop and think about it, we're pretty familiar, pretty comfortable, with being angry.

This is something we need to deal with, not just tolerate. The Bible has many warnings for us about anger, especially in Proverbs.[11] Scripture is clear that anger is an issue we need to not only keep an eye on but deal with quickly and thoroughly.

ANGER IN THE BIBLE

In the Sermon on the Mount, Jesus addressed anger specifically, shedding light on the New Covenant approach to the law. The Jews of Jesus' day were undoubtedly familiar with "Thou shalt not murder" and "Thou shalt not commit adultery." In speaking to these commandments, Jesus made it clear that anger is the seed of murder, and that anger expressed in seemingly innocent verbal outbursts still leaves us deserving judgment (Matthew 5:21–26).

Under the law in the Mosaic Covenant, when someone committed murder it needed to be dealt with by the community. But in the New Covenant, Jesus calls us to recognize the seed of murder in our own hearts and deal with it then, rather than let it grow to the point that it openly manifests as murder.

Remember Cain and Abel? In Genesis 4, Abel brought a sacrifice that pleased the Lord, and Cain did not. It bothered Cain and God called him out on it:

> Why are you *angry*, and why has your face fallen? If you do well, will you not be accepted? And if you do not do well, sin is crouching at the door. Its desire is contrary to you, *but you must rule over it.* (Genesis 4:6–7, emphasis added)

God warned Cain that his anger opened the door to sin and he needed to rule over it, to not be controlled by his anger but to get his anger under control.

---

[11] For example, see Proverbs 14:29, 16:32, 19:11, 22:24–25, 29:8, 22, and Ecclesiastes 7:9.

We work the muscle of controlling our anger in the small things—when we're cut off in traffic, when a child or employee disobeys, when something happens that's out of our control and throws a wrench into our plans. We process the frustration and cast it on the Lord, bringing it to Him and learning to leave it at His feet. If we don't learn to do this in the day-to-day, we're more likely to fail when the stakes are higher. We must learn to exercise self-control over our anger and frustration.

Consider this common principle of sin: it starts small, but it grows as we tolerate it. A small frustration is easy to explain away. But as we entertain that frustration, and another one, and another one, they soon develop into an offence. Offences that aren't dealt with start to leak out in our words and tone. And the longer they're left unchecked, the more bitter and angry we become. That bitter offence will lead us to do things we wouldn't otherwise imagine ourselves doing.

The same principle is at work in the command not to commit adultery. Adultery starts in the heart when we tolerate a wandering eye and entertain lustful thoughts. When left unchecked, it grows. Nobody jumps straight to murder or adultery; that would be unthinkable. But hundreds of baby steps in the wrong direction lead us to contemplate the unthinkable until suddenly it makes sense.

This is the point James makes in his letter.

> But each person is tempted when he is lured and enticed by his own desire. Then desire when it has conceived gives birth to sin, and sin when it is fully grown brings forth death. (James 1:14–15)

When we don't rule over our desires in the temptation phase, they give birth to sin, which works to produce death within us as we allow it to mature.

Making a priority of reading and meditating on the Word can help. As we read on in James 1:21, he implores his readers to receive the implanted word with meekness and allow it to save their souls, pointing out that only those who do what the Word teaches are blessed. We don't just read the Word and assume it will correct our anger issues. We must do the work of doing what the Word says.

James taught that looking into the Word, *"the perfect law"* (James 1:25), is like looking in the mirror in the morning. We can take a quick glance and move along without addressing any of the issues the mirror reveals. If we do that, we go about our day thinking we're shipshape, but that's not what everyone around us sees.

On the other hand, when we take the time to look more closely, we can see what needs to be washed, trimmed, or improved. We make ourselves more presentable for the day.

In the same way, we must persevere in looking into the Word and allow it to reveal our flaws and imperfections. This requires some humility and honesty, being willing to recognize the imperfections that will surely be revealed. Once aware of these imperfections, we can dialogue with the Holy Spirit on those matters and move toward change. We begin to exercise the spiritual fruit of self-control in dealing with those issues.

But it's about more than just becoming aware of our imperfections; we are to behold the perfections—the beauty—of Jesus in those same areas. When we do, the Word says that we are transformed into His image, from one degree of glory to another (2 Corinthians 3:18). We don't just resist being angry but set our hearts and minds to become more like Him in His gentleness.[12]

We must look into the Word, receive what its mirror shows us, and respond accordingly. Otherwise we profess a form of godliness but deny its power in our lives (2 Timothy 3:1–5).

OUR CHIEF EXAMPLE OF BEING SLOW TO ANGER

This is more than behaviour modification or skills we exercise. Being slow to anger must be an internal reality, a character trait of those who follow Jesus. Why? Because we are called to be as He is in this world (1

---

[12] For example, Jesus described Himself as *"gentle and lowly in heart"* (Matthew 11:29). Meditating on His gentleness starts to erode our anger. In this way, being transformed into His image is synonymous with growing in the fruit of the Spirit (Galatians 5:22–23).

John 4:17). Like the moon to the sun, we are to be reflections of the light of His character in the world around us. And being slow to anger is at the core of who He is.

At Mount Sinai, Moses pleaded with God not to move the Israelites on unless His presence would go with them. In that prayer, Moses boldly asked to see God's glory. God called Moses up onto the mountain the next day, and in that encounter He passed by Moses and proclaimed His name to him:

> The Lord, the Lord, a God merciful and gracious, *slow to anger,* and abounding in steadfast love and faithfulness, keeping steadfast love for thousands, forgiving iniquity and transgression and sin, but who will by no means clear the guilty… (Exodus 34:6–7, emphasis added)

There it is, right at the beginning of the declaration of who He is. He is slow to anger.

Dane Ortlund shares a powerful observation in his book, *Gentle and Lowly*. He acknowledges the many Old Testament examples of God being provoked to anger, examples which people use to argue that God Himself is angry.

But these statements actually reveal the opposite. We never read that He is provoked to mercy or lovingkindness, because those are His default responses. He doesn't need to be provoked to love because He *is* love.

On the other hand, being slow to anger means that His anger must be provoked in order to make an appearance. It doesn't show up readily but must be drawn out.[13]

Do you see the difference?

We, on the other hand, are not slow to anger. Anger comes easily to us. We are warned many times in the New Testament not to provoke each other or our children to anger, because our anger is so easily stirred. But what is the thing we need to be provoked to do?

---

[13] Dane Ortlund, *Gentle and Lowly* (Wheaton, IL: Crossway, 2020). From the audio edition.

> And let us consider how to stir up one another to love
> and good works… (Hebrews 10:24)

Anger is easy for us to tap into. It's the love and good works that we need to be provoked into.

God has called us to become like Him. This language first showed up in Leviticus 11:44, where God charged Israel to *"be holy, for I am holy,"* in the context of discussing ceremonial laws.

Jesus picked up on that statement and reiterated it in a very interesting teaching. When we continue reading the Sermon on the Mount, at the end of Matthew 5, He teaches us to love our enemies. Who stirs up our anger better than an enemy? Jesus tells us we are to forego—not indulge—our anger, instead loving and praying for the very ones who make our blood boil. He not only gives us that command, but He also gives us the reason: those who love their enemies show themselves to be sons of their Father in heaven, and this is one way in which we become perfect as He is perfect (Matthew 5:45, 48).

Catch what Jesus is saying: when we can control our anger by loving the ones who would stir it up, we start to look like Him. This is especially true in situations when we're in the right, holding the hammer of truth in the argument.

I think of situations in which a brother or leader wrongs us or someone we love. Does justice need to be realized? Definitely. Do repentance and perhaps restitution need to take place to make things right? Yes, one hundred percent.

But that doesn't give us Christ-followers permission to let our anger off the leash. Though we may be on the right side of the argument, when we add our anger as fuel to the fire, we short-circuit the process of establishing justice.

Did you catch what James said about our anger, and why we need to have a longer fuse?

> …for the anger of man does not produce the
> righteousness of God. (James 1:20)

Feel the weight of that statement: human anger isn't capable of producing the righteousness of God. It easily crosses the line into vengeance. Being right and walking it out properly are two very different things. As Jesus demonstrated on the cross, our goal is to love and pray for even the ones who have done us wrong.

This is who He is. He is slow to anger. It's in the family DNA. Every believer on earth, when wronged, is called to get a handle on their propensity for anger and learn to respond with love and blessing. Until we can do that, we don't yet truly reflect Him in this world.

In Luke 9:51–56, Jesus is training two of His inner circle disciples in this matter. On their way to Jerusalem, Jesus sent messengers ahead into a Samaritan village, announcing that He was on His way through and would visit. But the village wasn't interested in hosting Him. The Son of God Himself offered to roll into town with all His miracles and signs and wonders—and they declined.

The two sons of Zebedee didn't take the rejection well, and they asked Jesus for permission to call down fire from heaven to destroy the town. They even had biblical precedent for this idea, from the life of Elijah (2 Kings 1).

But Jesus rebuked them, decisively shutting down their idea. Some versions say that He added, *"You do not know what kind of spirit you are"* (Luke 9:55, NASB). That's kind of like Jesus saying, "You guys haven't figured out what We're about yet. We don't work like that."

Like John and his brother James, we are sometimes eager to find examples in Scripture that give us permission to vent our anger. You might already have two or three scriptural examples of righteous anger in mind as you read this.

But let's not forget that the overwhelming message in Scripture is that we should keep our anger in check. This teaching is sprinkled throughout Paul's letters, with reminders to always speak graciously, live lives of demonstrable gentleness, and understand that the Kingdom of God is primarily recognized by righteousness, peace, and joy in the Holy Spirit—opposites of anger and judgment (Colossians 4:6, Philippians 4:5, Romans 14:17).

We also do well to remember that unchecked anger was behind the reason Moses didn't get to enter the Promised Land, even after leading Israel with faithfulness and humility through their forty years in the wilderness.

Rather than looking for justification to be angry, we should receive all that Scripture clearly has to say about being gracious and gentle.

Think of the fruit of the Spirit in Galatians 5, the nine wonderful attributes of God that Paul said would be evident in the lives of Spirit-filled believers. Anger stands in direct contrast to every facet of this fruit. Moreover, Paul categorized varying expressions of anger as fruits of the flesh, including hostility, quarrelling, jealousy, outbursts of anger, selfish ambition, dissension, and division (Galatians 5:19–21).

Anger is the opposite of the fruit of the Spirit; it is the fruit of our flesh. We are instructed to make no provision for the flesh, but instead to subject it to the cross and put it to death (Romans 13:14, Galatians 5:24, Colossians 3:5–8). Anger is not to have a consistent presence in the life of the believer.

I understand that there are examples of righteous anger in Scripture. Like declarations and decrees in the last chapter, these expressions only bear good fruit when they're initiated by the Lord. That's the tricky part: discerning what is truly righteous anger, and what is ours. It's a difficult task because we can easily be convinced that a strong emotion is the leading of the Lord. It's incredibly important for us to learn to discern the difference rightly, because James very clearly states that the anger of man will not produce the righteousness of God (James 1:20).

No matter how righteous or noble the cause, if we act or speak out of our own anger, we build something that is contrary to the Kingdom of God. If we truly want to see His Kingdom come and His will be done in Canada, we need to be in line with how He establishes His Kingdom.

We'll explore this more later, but for now I'll point to Isaiah 42:1–7 as a picture of how Jesus went about demonstrating His will and bringing His Kingdom to bear during His earthly ministry. Expressions of righteous anger are most certainly the exception, whereas humility and meekness are the rule of the Kingdom.

AN UNHOLY FASCINATION WITH JUDGMENT

Many unbelievers in our culture today have a negative view of the church. We'd like to believe it's because of the offence of the gospel, but numerous surveys suggest that it has more to do with our conduct. We tend to be known for standing against things we disagree with—often angrily, at that—rather than standing for what we value. A common caricature of the modern Christian might be a grumpy face paired with a judgmental, complaining, even whiny voice. That certainly doesn't describe Jesus, the One we are to be emulating!

If we're honest, we have a bit of the same angry, reactionary thinking that John and James once had. Something in our flesh wants to see others punished for wrongdoing. This is cancel culture in a nutshell; we demand retribution when someone is exposed for doing something heinous. We call it justice, but it's really about exacting a pound of flesh.

Somewhere along the line, this vindictive nature has been falsely attributed to God. Many people, believers and unbelievers alike, think God angrily keeps an eye on the sons of men, looking for opportunities to judge. It is absolutely true that He is a just Judge and will not rest until He has established justice on earth. But we seem to forget that Jesus demonstrated the just Judge to also be a Bridegroom who is motivated by love, or a good Shepherd who is gentle and lowly in heart.

In His late-night conversation with Nicodemus, Jesus gave us the quote that most people would point to as the gospel in a nutshell—John 3:16. But the following verse is equally important, because it gives us the motivation behind His coming: *"For God did not send his Son into the world to condemn the world, but in order that the world might be saved through him"* (John 3:17, emphasis added). His first motivation is to save and restore the relationship that was broken at the fall and reconcile us to God (2 Corinthians 5:11–21). The why is just as important as the what.

We see that intention to show mercy in His first coming, but did you know we can see it in the second coming as well?

In 2 Peter 3, Peter describes the generation of the Lord's return. He encourages the believers to remain steadfast in the face of scoffing and persecution, knowing that the Lord will fulfill His promise to return and purge the earth of sin and wickedness with fire. It's admittedly heavy on the judgment theme.

Peter acknowledges the argument of scoffers we still hear today: "Where is He? It's been thousands of years and life carries on as it always has. What makes you believe this generation will be any different?" But he warns against being lured to sleep by that argument. We think God is slow to fulfill His promises, but Peter points us to what's truly happening: *"The Lord is not slow… but is <u>patient toward you</u>, <u>not wishing that any should perish, but that all should reach repentance</u>"* (2 Peter 3:9, emphasis added).

We assume that God is like us. He sees something He doesn't like, snaps, and that's it. But He is slow to anger. He is the most self-controlled in all the universe. He offers mankind multiple opportunities to repent, having endured our collective sin for thousands of years. And lest we think that His slowness to anger is dispassionate or frustrated, some translations, like the King James Version, translate it as longsuffering. He patiently endures with humanity in its sin, restraining the wrath that justice demands to give people more time to turn. And He does that at a great personal cost.

We see this longsuffering in the parable of the tenants (Matthew 21:33–34). Jesus describes God's history of sending messenger after messenger to warn and turn hearts, culminating in the sending of His only begotten Son. We see it again as He lamented over Jerusalem, knowing that His people were about to put Him to death, yet He still looked forward to the day when they would say, *"Blessed is he who comes in the name of the Lord"* (Matthew 23:39).

God isn't looking for excuses to strike people with lightning! The opposite is true: He is slow to anger.

We even see this in the judgments of the book of Revelation. Some view them as cruel punishment, even torture, but there is mercy in them. Each judgment represents another shaking, another warning, another opportunity to turn.

John sadly notes that many who survive the seven seals and the first six trumpet judgments remain stubborn in their hearts, refusing to repent of their sinful deeds, idolatry, murder, sorcery, immorality, and theft (Revelation 9:20–21). Each successive judgment is another opportunity for mankind to realize they are standing on the wrong side and humble themselves, repent, and turn to the Lord before the end of the age. That is merciful!

In the big picture, judgments are a warning, opportunities for mankind to become aware of eternity and get right with Him.

God never suspends one attribute to express another.[14] He doesn't ignore His holiness and justice when He lavishes love on us, nor does He put away mercy when dealing with our sin. He is zealous to establish justice and righteousness on the earth, but He is simultaneously slow to anger and desires that none should perish as He sovereignly moves human history toward the end of the age.

The prophet Jonah could serve as a litmus test for our own hearts in this matter. The giant fish that housed Jonah for three days gets most of the attention in this story, but what happened in Nineveh through Jonah's ministry is quite remarkable. He walked through the enormous city, declaring that it was going to be overthrown in forty days. It's interesting to note that there was no call to repentance, no invitation to turn. Just "God says your time is up."

Think of how doomsday prophets on street corners are received today. Most passersby pay them no attention, and any attention they do give is usually of the unkind variety. But the entire city of Nineveh, including its king, voluntarily responded to Jonah's similar message with fasting and repentance—and without being told to! Hear the faith and desperation of the Assyrian king in his decree: *"Let everyone call urgently on God… Who knows? God may yet relent and with compassion turn from his fierce anger so that we will not perish"* (Jonah 3:8–9, NIV).

In response to this repentance, God relented.

These are the same people who would, in a few decades' time, destroy the northern kingdom of Israel. They were an empire renowned for cruelty and brutality. Yet God delighted to show even them mercy when they turned in repentance.

---

[14] A.W. Tozer, *The Knowledge of the Holy* (San Francisco, CA: HarperCollins, 1961), 98.

Perhaps even more shocking than the miraculous response to Jonah's preaching is Jonah's own response to it in the fourth chapter. You would think he'd be thrilled at how people responded to his message, but he was angry at God for being gracious, merciful, slow to anger, and abounding in love. Jonah had *wanted* God to destroy Nineveh! He was so angry about it that he became suicidal, literally asking God to end his life. Jonah hoped for God to judge the Assyrians, even going so far as to build a hut on a nearby hillside to have a front row seat for the destruction in case God changed His mind.

It's interesting to note that God appears to deal gently with Jonah in correcting him. We don't know how Jonah's heart ended up after this whole event, but it's clear that he was hoping for God to act in judgment. Unfortunately for him, God was happy to relent from doing harm when the people of Nineveh responded with repentance.

We need to ask ourselves, "Am I like Jonah?" While it's plain to see unrighteousness advancing in our land, I would suggest that hoping and praying for judgment is not where we should start. After all, 1 Peter 4:17 tells us that judgment starts with the household of God. If we're going to ask God to call unrighteousness to account—to shake everything that can be shaken—we must be ready to have our own lives measured by the same standard. Indeed, it seems like that process may have already begun in the Western church.

It's important to remember that our battle is not with flesh and blood, but with powers, principalities, and evil spirits at work around us (Ephesians 6:12). To vent anger at the people perpetrating unrighteousness is to miss the target—they are the very ones God desires to lead to repentance!

INTERCESSION OR ACCUSATION?

In the Bible, we encounter two figures with competing ministries before the throne of God.

On the one hand, we see the ministry of intercession in Jesus, our great High Priest. He is seated at the right hand of God and lives to make intercession for us (Hebrews 7:25, Romans 8:34, Isaiah 53:12). I love this facet of Jesus' ministry!

On the other hand, we see a ministry of accusation, headlined by Satan. His activity is clearly referenced in Revelation 12:10, which tells us that he accuses believers before God.[15] He constantly reminds God of our sins, faults, weaknesses, and failures.

We see a glimpse of how he works in the first two chapters of Job, where he argued before God that Job wasn't truly faithful to Him, because he had such an easy, prosperous life. He accused Job's character, calling him something of a fair-weather follower of God.

Satan accused Job then, and he accuses us today. You may have noticed that he also accuses God to you, trying to convince you that God has forgotten you, rejected you, or is fed up with your constant stumbling. It's just what he does.

With these two ministries in mind, let me ask a question: when you pray for your enemies or those in authority over you, which ministry do you participate in? Do your prayers align with Christ's ministry of intercession, or do they sound more like accusations? Do your prayers express a desire to see those people fail, or to see them experience the goodness of God? Whose prayers do you echo before the throne: those of the great Intercessor or those of the accuser?

Yes, God is grieved at the proliferation of sin and unrighteousness in our day. Yes, He sometimes steps into time and space to deal with the sin of mankind in His sovereignty. But I'm seeking to draw attention to the posture of our hearts in all this. Do we inwardly long to see God move in judgment toward those who disagree with us or potentially persecute us, like Jonah? Or is our desire to see the grace and mercy of God win out in those people's lives while there's still time?

Believe it or not, it is possible for us to stand for truth and justice without harbouring hatred or anger toward people who vehemently oppose God. This especially concerns how we pray for governments we perceive to be in opposition to the Kingdom of God.

Daniel is a phenomenal example of how to do this. He was taken into exile by King Nebuchadnezzar of Babylon, removed from the

---

[15] Note that the word "devil" references an accuser or slanderer.

ESSENTIAL #3: BE SLOW *to* ANGER

world he knew as a young man, and indoctrinated into the philosophy, religion, and culture of his new country. The Babylonians attempted to systematically scrub all traces of Judaism from his life. Daniel had every right to be angry at this new king and resist his kingdom.

Despite all this, we have no evidence that he ever rebelled against Nebuchadnezzar, nor any of the successive kings he served. In fact, the opposite is true: he served them with an excellent spirit, honoured them faithfully, and wished for their health and well-being (Daniel 4:19, 5:14, 6:3–4, 21–22). He did this all while remaining faithful to His God.

If anyone had an excuse to harbour anger against the government, it was Daniel. Yet he demonstrated no anger or offence toward the kings he served. More importantly, that lack of anger doesn't appear to have harmed his witness.

Does that mean he was never frustrated or angered by things they said or did? Not at all likely. But it does mean that Daniel was able to rule over that anger and offence, preventing them from taking root in his heart. He didn't allow bitterness to compromise his ability to serve God with integrity and excellence, even when that service was done in the courts of evil, arrogant, demon-worshiping kings.

Do you want to know what God thought of this man who faithfully served those wicked kings? Check out how He talked about Daniel to his contemporary, Ezekiel. He pointed to Daniel as a standard of righteousness and wisdom in Ezekiel 14 and 28. Not to mention, Daniel is called *"greatly beloved"* in two separate encounters (Daniel 9:23, 10:11, 19). To put it in Jesus' words, Daniel was a true son of his Father in heaven.

Human anger most commonly comes from a place of fear, not righteousness, and we know that He has not given us a spirit of fear (Romans 8:15, 2 Timothy 1:7). Any time we have the urge to pray or decree about the government from a place of anger, it's a good time to pause and ask, "Why am I angry?" Is it truly because of a sense of the Lord's name being blasphemed, or is it possibly related to the fear of a loss of familiar freedoms, benefits, or comforts?

There are some who pray for governments to fall or be overthrown. No matter what kind of spiritual face we put on it, such prayer is typically rooted in anxiety and fear. I believe this type of prayer for government is directly linked to a low view of the sovereignty of God.

Think about it. Daniel 2:21 tells us that God removes some kings and elevates others. So when we pray for our government to fall, we must have arrived at one of three conclusions:

1. This government somehow came to power outside of the sovereignty of God, and God needs to get things back in order.

2. God brought them to power, but that was a mistake, and we need to fix it *now*.

3. Democracy has produced a freewill loophole, and Daniel 2:21 no longer applies today.

All three of these conclusions are erroneous. If we truly stand on the Word and believe that He upholds all things by the word of His power, and that He removes kings and sets up others as He pleases (Hebrews 1:3, Daniel 2:21), what do we have to be fearful or anxious about? We know that one day He will come and unseat every earthly government (Daniel 7:13–14, Revelation 11:15), holding leaders accountable for how they have led. Until then, we can continue to boldly pray for His Kingdom to come and His will to be done, no matter what government is in place.

Let's not forget that both Paul and Peter urged Christians to honour, submit to, and pray for those in authority over them (1 Timothy 2:1–4, Romans 13:1–7, Titus 3:1–2, 1 Peter 2:13–17). They said this about the very government and rulers who would make martyrs out of them both. This is completely in accordance with Jesus' teaching to love our enemies and pray for the ones who persecute us.

Does this mean we blindly agree with everything our government says and does? No, it does not. In Daniel 6, Daniel faithfully observed his practice of praying to the Lord three times daily, even though it went against the law of the land. But he never lashed out against the king or carried a vendetta in his heart toward him; in fact, when King Darius opened the lions' den the morning after throwing him in, Daniel greeted him:

> *O king, live forever!* My God sent his angel and shut the lions' mouths, and they have not harmed me, because I was found blameless before him; and *also before you, O king, I have done no harm.* (Daniel 6:21–22, emphasis added)

You see, it is possible to resist unrighteous laws, remain faithful to God, yet still bless and honour the government that created those same laws.

I don't know of any passages of Scripture that give us permission to put the fruit of the Spirit on the shelf and indulge in the fruits of the flesh, not even when the government does something we don't agree with.

In North America we have the privilege of living in a political system that gives us the opportunity to have a say in how we are governed. If we don't like the way our country is governed, we must acknowledge a hard truth: perhaps we have not sufficiently engaged in the political process freely afforded to us. If our country is moving in a direction we don't like, maybe we need to evaluate whether we are effectively being salt and light.

Evangelicals used to carry influence across the political spectrum in Canada, but for some reason many of us, though not all, have huddled over to the right and abandoned the posts on the left. Let's be clear about something: no political party in Canada can be called the party of the Kingdom of God. The salt and light of the Kingdom needs to be present across the board and on both sides of the aisle.

This won't miraculously change in one election cycle, even with the election of a preferred leader. The political change we desire will only come with the steady, consistent influence of believers who bear the fruit of the Spirit, being salt and light in every sphere of society for years to come.

Our political fortunes have not changed overnight, nor should we expect them be restored in that timeframe. The truth is that if our hope for change is wrapped up in the political system and election cycles, we have succumbed to a political spirit. Jesus referred to that as the leaven of Herod (Mark 8:15).

ANOTHER WAY TO PRAY

Let's get back to the subject of prayer. If we're struggling with frustration and anxiety over the direction in which our nation is moving, Paul has an instruction for us.

In Philippians, he encouraged a church that was politically and socially excluded from society. He knew they carried fears, concerns, and anxieties related to these exclusions, as they had a real impact on everyday life. So he reminded them that they were first citizens of heaven, not Philippi or Rome. Read how he encouraged them:

> *Rejoice* in the Lord always; again I will say, rejoice. Let your reasonableness [gentleness] be known to everyone. The Lord is at hand; *do not be anxious* about anything, but in everything by prayer and supplication *with thanksgiving* let your requests be made known to God. And the peace of God, which surpasses all understanding, will guard your hearts and your minds in Christ Jesus. (Philippians 4:4–7, emphasis added)

Paul gave the Philippians a clear invitation not to let fear, anxiety, or frustration rule them. Instead he encouraged them to carry themselves with reasonableness (gentleness) toward everyone in town. In the place of prayer, he encouraged them to start with thanksgiving.

When you are upset about the direction our country appears to be moving in, first get your eyes back on the One who is seated on the throne by way of thanksgiving. Remember His omnipresence, omnipotence, and omniscience. Remember that He is the good Shepherd who makes all things work together for good. Let thanksgiving and praise spill out. Then make your requests known to God. You'll find the peace of God beginning to guard your heart and mind, and your prayers will start to sound more like Christ's intercession than Satan's accusation.

We've seen this happen within our little sphere at NHOP. Like most, we typically prayed for our government from a place of concern and frustration over legislation, policy, tactics, and so on. But as we studied James, our hearts changed. Does the government still say and do things that tick us off? Definitely. But we no longer see politicians as adversaries. We're starting to see them as the ones Christ willingly gave up His life for, because He desires that they be with Him.

One thing the Holy Spirit has challenged us to do is pray for these ministers as though they were our sons and daughters. That has completely upended how we pray. We don't pray for the downfall of prodigals; we pray for their eyes to open and their hearts to return!

I want to share that challenge with you. When you pray for our prime minister, or for your riding's MP, posture your heart to pray for them as though you were praying for your own child or parent. You'll likely discover what we've found, that we're no longer angrily fixated on the latest bill or political stunt. Instead we constantly remember and call on His sovereignty and goodness. And here's an added bonus: we've found that this kind of prayer is a lot more sustainable.

What's exciting about this is that God is giving us eyes to see where He's moving. He hasn't abandoned Canada, as some might suggest. When we fixate on what's going wrong, we have a harder time seeing what He's up to. But when we keep our eyes on Him, we can see what He's doing. We're filled with faith and expectation for what He's going to do next, and that fuels us to pray more!

There are very concerning trends in Canada today. Psalm 2 describes a generation of rulers and people who actively resist the leadership of God, even raging against Him, His ways, and His chosen Ruler. In some ways, Canada seems to be a global leader in this unholy charge. But we must not lose sight of what He has said:

> For behold, darkness shall cover the earth, and thick darkness the peoples; *but the Lord will arise upon*

you, and his glory will be seen upon you. (Isaiah 60:2, emphasis added)

He has promised that His light will outshine darkness, and church history tells us that He has been faithful to that promise. Keep your eyes on Him and what He's doing, because He will display His glory in and through us, no matter how dark the darkness gets (Romans 8:35–39, Revelation 12:11, 2 Corinthians 4:6–12, Matthew 13:24–30).

James writes that the anger of man doesn't produce the righteousness of God (James 1:20). It just doesn't. Even if in response to a noble cause, the presence of our anger in the roots will mean the fruit isn't good. God is slow to anger, and we are to be as He is in this world.

When we read on, we find that James offered a conclusion to this thought. He didn't just tell us that the anger of man fails to produce the righteousness of God; he showed us what does: *"Peacemakers who sow in peace reap a harvest of righteousness"* (James 3:18, NIV)

If we want to pray in and reap a harvest of righteousness in Canada, we must commit to laying aside our anger and becoming peacemakers.

ESSENTIAL #4

Pray with Impartiality (James 2:1–13)

My brothers, show no partiality…
if you show partiality, you are committing sin…
(James 2:1, 9)

As we move into the second chapter of James, let's recap what we've observed so far. James encourages us to be quick to listen and slow to speak, to spend a little more time in thinking and reflection before talking. He encourages us to exercise self-control instead of venting our anger, which also implies more thinking and reflection and less reactionary speech. He ties these ideas together by encouraging us to look into the Word diligently, receiving its correction and instruction and putting into practice what it says.

He also likens the Word to a mirror. When we simply read the Word and move along, it's like taking only a passing glance at the mirror in the morning. You think you know what you look like, but you immediately forget what the mirror showed you and the imperfections it revealed. To persevere in looking into the Word is to pay attention to what the mirror shows you, doing what the Word says and making changes. The Word shows us the areas where His character has not yet been formed in us. If we let it do its work, it will make us a truer reflection of Him in the world.

On the heels of this encouragement, James wastes no time putting a spotlight on the first blemish he sees: partiality. He calls out the practice of giving preferential treatment to the rich, well-dressed, and honourable while treating the poor as an afterthought in Christian gatherings. He reminds us to love our neighbours as ourselves (James 2:8), adding that if we truly live that way, we are doing well. But treating some people better than others is the opposite of what Jesus taught, and James plainly calls it a sin (James 2:9).

He clearly applies his point to the discrepancy between how we tend to treat the rich and the poor. We could certainly expand on this, but we're going to take a closer look at the plight of the poor in the next chapter. As we laid out in the introduction, we're looking at how James' teachings apply to how we pray.

US VS. THEM

We seem to have an innate need to categorize everything and everyone. There's something simple, perhaps comforting, about being able to draw quick conclusions. Any unknown leads to unease. We like to know where others fit on our grid. Do they think like us? Believe what we believe? Like what we like? Are they safe? We look for indicators, especially in their vocabulary, to give us clues as to whether they belong in our camp.

With that information, we attach a label to them, soothing some of our anxiety. We're very good at this. Thanks to the internet, we can now draw conclusions about others without having a single interaction with them.

This has become a big issue in our society today, especially with the rise of identity politics. An ever-widening chasm is developing between the left and right, with the middle ground rapidly disappearing. If you take all your cues from the media, it seems there is no more left or right, but only the radical left and far right. I've read articles by those who've identified as moderates for years, but now they find themselves labelled as extremists or fascists. Many families have completely fallen apart over differences in political ideology. As already mentioned, these chasms only widened under the pressures of the COVID years.

Lest we think this is a world problem and not a church problem, consider this. Do we not identify ourselves more by what differentiates us than by what unites us? We're Calvinist or Arminian, cessationist or continuationist, complementarian or egalitarian. We're Baptist,

ESSENTIAL #4: PRAY *with* IMPARTIALITY

Methodist, Presbyterian, Charismatic, Lutheran, Pentecostal, Catholic, nondenominational, etc.

Paul clearly spoke against this way of thinking in 1 Corinthians 3. The Corinthians categorized themselves according to which apostolic ministry they followed. Paul responded by reminding them that we are not to define ourselves by who planted or watered the seed of the Kingdom in our lives, but by the God who made the seed grow. No matter what stream you follow, no matter which teachers you listen to, we are all built on the same foundation of Jesus Christ (1 Corinthians 3:7, 11). Shouldn't we start there?

When we keep our differences front of mind, we tend to gravitate toward the people who see things the way we do and avoid the ones who see differently. In extreme cases, we attack and insult those on the opposite side of the debate. YouTube is littered with videos of people throwing stones at teachers based on five-second soundbites often taken out of context.

The sad reality is that a simple fact-check would often show the accusation to be misguided. It's very easy to deny someone the benefit of the doubt and presume them guilty if they're not from the same stream as us. While love is supposed to hope and believe all things, we're quick to assume the worst of others. Once again, it's good to be quick to listen and slow to speak.[16]

Scripture is clear about the fact that partiality is not in God's character. He shows no racial prejudice, which is evidenced by the assembled throng around His throne from every tribe, tongue, people, and ethnicity (Revelation 5:9). Jesus, the express image of the Father, was not nervous around the poor, the demonically possessed and oppressed, the deformed, or the diseased. He wasn't afraid of associating with sinners and tax collectors—all the "others" (Luke 5:12–13, 6:6–11, 8:26–39, Matthew 11:19).

Jesus even brought some of these messy divisions right into His inner circle. Matthew was a Jew who had become a Roman tax collec-

---

[16] I'm not suggesting that Christians should ignore discernment and cease to hold teachers accountable for wrong teachings. I am suggesting that there might be a better way to go about doing that than our current culture of heresy hunting.

tor. Simon was a Zealot, Jewish revolutionaries of the day who were opposed to Roman rule and taxation. They were known to carry concealed daggers, which they used to murder men they considered to be enemies of Israel, including turncoat tax collectors.[17] Jesus brought tax collector Matthew and his would-be assassin into the same small group and not only made them get along but taught them to love each other.

While God isn't uncomfortable with people who might make us uncomfortable, He also isn't wowed by anyone we're impressed by. Elihu, the only friend of Job's who spoke rightly of God, said this: *"He doesn't care how great a person may be, and he pays no more attention to the rich than to the poor. He made them all"* (Job 34:19, NLT). God isn't impressed by human talent, status, or wisdom. Nobody gets preferential treatment from Him because no one is righteous or wise before Him. He judges all with justice and equity (Acts 10:34, Romans 2:11, Galatians 2:6, Isaiah 64:6, Romans 3:20–23, Proverbs 29:13, Job 38–31, Psalm 67:4, 96:10, 98:9, 99:4, Isaiah 11:4).

Just as we are to be slow to anger, like Him, we are to be impartial as He is impartial. We are to honour the ones who are beneath us on whatever socioeconomic scale we measure by, and we are not to show special fear or privilege to the ones who are above us (Leviticus 19:15, Deuteronomy 1:17, 16:19, Job 13:10, Proverbs 18:5, 24:23, Malachi 2:9, 1 Timothy 5:21, 1 Corinthians 12:22–24).

We give honour where honour is due, but we don't stand in awe of man. This is the standard we are called to. We are to treat the poor as well as we treat the rich, the Liberal as the Conservative, the Baptist as the Pentecostal, and so on.

WHO DO WE PRAY FOR?

Here's the question: do you show partiality in your prayer life? Do you only pray for people who think like you? Believe what you believe? Vote like you vote?

---

[17] F.F. Bruce, "Zealot," "Assassin," *New Bible Dictionary* (Downers Grove, IL: Intervarsity Press, 1996).

ESSENTIAL #4: PRAY *with* IMPARTIALITY

We at NHOP noticed a very interesting trend concerning this question a few years ago. We were established in 2004 with the vision of being an embassy of prayer in our nation's capital. Our building, a former monastery, was outfitted with dozens of bedrooms, which allowed us to welcome intercessors from across Canada to come and pray for our nation, mere blocks from Parliament Hill. Those who came could visit Parliament Hill, arrange to meet their MP, and participate in prayer times with believers who had come from other parts of the country for the same purpose.

For the first ten years or so, NHOP enjoyed a steady stream of people coming from across Canada to join with us in lifting our government in prayer.

Then came the federal election of 2015. Justin Trudeau's Liberal party was victorious, and Stephen Harper's Conservatives were ousted. The curious thing is that the flow of visiting intercessors from around the country slowed significantly after that election.

Do you see the problem? This is a big red flag.

Politically, the evangelical church seems to have this notion that the Conservative party is the official party of the Kingdom of God in Canada, like the Republican Party in the U.S. It is not. The Conservatives do have some policies that align with Kingdom values, but they have many others that don't. We can easily overlook that the NDP appear to show more concern for the poor than the Conservatives, and the poor are front and centre in God's heart.[18]

No single political party in Canada is the answer to the prayer *"Your kingdom come, your will be done, on earth as it is in heaven"* (Matthew 6:10). Because of that, I believe we cannot make the case that one party deserves to be prayed for more than the others.

Like Joshua learned on the plains of Jericho, God isn't subject to our structures and constructs. He isn't forced to pick which political party He approves of. He is on His own side, and it's our job to be in line with Him.

Sometimes it's easy to think, "If we could just get a Christian prime minister elected, if we could just pass some Christian laws, if we could

---

[18] More on that in the next chapter.

just…" Whether or not we recognize it, such thinking puts our hope in politics and political leaders. But we already have our Messiah!

Again, the Kingdom of God will not come to fruition in Canada because of the efforts or policies of a political party. There are no political saviours for the church, so we shouldn't set our hopes on one.

An overview of the Old Testament shows us that a good government is no guarantee that the nation has turned, or will turn, to the Lord.

Judah was taken into exile shortly after the passing of King Josiah, one of the few "good" kings in their history. Though they had the benefit of Josiah's reign and reforms, not to mention Jeremiah's prophetic ministry, the people remained distant from God. Though they had good laws, the heart of the nation didn't change.

The law has never produced righteousness or worked salvation in the hearts of men (Galatians 2:16, Romans 3:9–12, 20), yet we somehow think that a change in legislation will make Canada a truly Christian nation. In His earthly ministry, Jesus never sought a political platform to help advance His Kingdom agenda. In the same way, we shouldn't look to politics as the means of advancing the Kingdom.

One of the most often quoted verses of encouragement is found in Jeremiah 29:11: *"For I know the plans I have for you, declares the Lord, plans for welfare and not for evil, to give you a future and a hope."* But have you ever looked closer to understand the context of this statement? It's from a letter Jeremiah wrote to the Jews who had been exiled to Babylon. Some among these exiles had been prophesying false hopes, telling the people to hang on because the Lord was surely going to change their political fortunes quickly.

What was the Lord actually saying? "Settle in. Put your roots down. Build homes, plant gardens, and grow your families. You're going to be in Babylon for a while… seventy years, in fact. You would be wise to contribute to the well-being of the city you're in, because as it goes for them, so it will go for you."

God's plans for His people were good, with a hope and a future, but that included settling down in exile for a lot longer than they had hoped. Notice that even in exile God was promising them fruitfulness: growing families, productive gardens, and peace. Yes, there was a promise of deliverance, but He was telling them not to sit around waiting for that deliverance to come. Using New Testament terminology, they were to focus on being salt and light in Babylon.

Keep in mind that this was all happening at the exact same time Daniel was serving in the courts of Nebuchadnezzar. He was faithfully doing the salt and light thing in the land of his exile, and in the courts of an arrogant, evil king.

Paul had similar messaging for some in Thessalonica who were waiting around for the second coming. He implored them to apply themselves and seek the welfare of their families and city (1 Thessalonians 4:11–12, 2 Thessalonians 3:6–12). We shouldn't wait around to be saved by a favourable election result—or the second coming, for that matter. We should be engaging and seeking the welfare of our cities, regions, provinces, and nation today.

Democratic governments are largely a reflection of the population who vote them in. The government doesn't change the hearts of the people; the hearts of the people determine the government. If the church in Canada would be an effective, faithful presence of salt and light in her communities across the country, we would be more likely to see a change in the political direction of our nation.

Let's return to the notion that the Conservatives are God's party in Canada. Even if this were true, Scripture is clear that we are not to be partial toward them. Again, let's recall Paul's words:

> First of all, then, I urge that supplications, prayers, intercessions, and thanksgivings be made for *all people, for kings and all who are in high positions,* that we may lead a peaceful and quiet life, godly and dignified in every way. This is good, and it is pleasing in the sight of God our Savior, who desires all people to be saved and to come to the knowledge of the truth. (1 Timothy 2:1–4, emphasis added)

Paul told Timothy to make sure that prayer was being offered on behalf of all people, all kings, and all who were in positions of authority—

not just the ones they liked or agreed with. Paul urged the churches to pray for Roman emperors who resisted the spread of the gospel, killed believers, and even demanded to be worshiped as deities themselves. It's safe to assume that Paul didn't agree with those emperors, yet he encouraged the church to pray for them.

When we read this passage, we often stop after the bit about leading a quiet and peaceful life. But notice what Paul adds: we pray for these leaders, especially those who don't know Him, because God's desire is that all would be saved and come to the knowledge of the truth. We don't just pray for our leaders so we'll have a comfortable life; we pray for them because God desires that even they would come to know Him. When we pray with the latter in mind, it is evidence that we are seeking first His Kingdom and righteousness above our own wants and needs.

We can apply this to our interactions within the body of Christ as well. I encourage you to pray not only for those in your local church and denomination, but the entire body of Christ. It's true that there are too many denominations and networks to count. And yes, it is good to pray focused, intentional prayers. Keep doing that.

But we also need to guard our hearts from treating one part of the body preferentially above the others. When a leader from a rival stream stumbles in a public failure, do we rejoice and gloat? Or do we pray earnestly for them, their families, and those in their care to experience the correction, healing, and restoration of the Lord? Do we extend them the same mercy and benefit of the doubt we would extend to a leader we trust and follow? We must remember that we are one body, not in competition with other streams. When one falls, we all take the hit (1 Corinthians 12:26).

Paul didn't just teach us to resist sectarianism, but that we should also pursue unity, making *"every effort to keep the unity of the Spirit through the bond of peace"* (Ephesians 4:3, NIV). Yes, we stand for truth and holiness, without compromise, but we need to find a way to do that without destroying the unity of the Spirit in the body.

It's important to remember that Jesus' final request before going to the cross was to have a church as unified as He was with the Father (John 17:20–23). We must find a way to grow, contend, and stand without breaking fellowship with others whose names are also written in the Lamb's book of life, even if they carry some different convictions than us.

MOVING AWAY FROM PARTIALITY

We must identify partiality as a mindset that's unwelcome in the Kingdom of God. James asserts that when we give preferential treatment to one person or group over another, we have *"made distinctions among [ourselves], and become judges with evil motives"* (James 2:4, NASB, emphasis added). We obviously don't want to be judges with evil motives before the Lord, so how do we move away from partiality in our lives?

There are three primary responses, all of which are good places to start.

Humility. If we return to Paul's comments in 1 Corinthians 3 and continue reading through chapter four, we see that arrogance feeds sectarianism, and by extension partiality. Of course, we believe what we believe because we think it's right, so a natural conclusion would be to assume that anyone who thinks differently from us is wrong.

But note what the great apostle Paul acknowledged:

> My conscience is clear, *but that doesn't prove that I'm right*. It is the Lord himself who will examine me and decide. So don't make judgments about anyone ahead of time—before the Lord returns. (1 Corinthians 4:4–5, NLT, emphasis added)

We don't know the whole truth just because we believe we do. We're only human, restricted in vision and finite in understanding. We don't see the whole picture. That's why we're in a body; we need each other!

But to walk with one another in this way, leaning on one another instead of fighting, we need to walk in humility.

> For by the grace given to me I say to *everyone among you not to think of himself more highly than he ought to think,*

> but to think with sober judgment, each according to the measure of faith that God has assigned. For as in one body we have many members, and the members do not all have the same function, so we, though many, are one body in Christ, and individually members one of another. (Romans 12:3–5, emphasis added)

We must discern whether partiality is at work in us, as it is arrogant and tribalistic at its core. Live with a clear conscience, following truth as best you know how, but resist the urge to judge those whose consciences have arrived at a different conviction. When we interact with fellow believers who have a different view, instead of immediately drawing conclusions, let's be like the Bereans, who are honoured in Scripture for how they eagerly and diligently searched the Scriptures daily to prove whether Paul's teachings were true (Acts 17:11).

Truth is not threatened by challenges. It's only strengthened by them. Don't be afraid of challenges to what you believe; the key is to let them drive you to search out the truth with even more diligence. We don't abandon truth for the sake of getting along, but we should be willing to acknowledge the possibility that we don't have it all figured out yet. If the apostle Paul can admit to that, we should be able to as well. Be willing to go to the Word again, asking the Holy Spirit who inspired its writing to come and reveal truth to us.

We should apply this humble approach to how we relate to believers from other streams and what they believe. A similar approach also works well in relating to people with different political views.

Mercy. Rather than looking down our noses at people who think differently than us, we should relate to them with kindness. We show mercy instead of judgment.

James wrote that we are to live with an awareness that we are going to be judged under the law of liberty, the law that sets us free (James 2:12). It's not that we won't be judged, but that we'll be judged by a very good and gracious standard.

But there is a responsibility attached to that standard: if we expect to receive mercy, we are expected to show mercy to others.

ESSENTIAL #4: PRAY *with* IMPARTIALITY

> *There will be no mercy for those who have not shown mercy to others.* But if you have been merciful, God will be merciful when he judges you. (James 2:13, NLT, emphasis added)

We often forget that it was the kindness of God that brought us to repentance. Why should we expect Him to deal differently with others? I love the way Preston Sprinkle puts it: "Paul said it's the kindness of God that leads to repentance (Romans 2:4). So if you really think someone should repent, how kind are you?"[19] We shouldn't get aggressive with people we disagree with. We should be kind.

When we hear people talk about God's unconditional love, we can find ourselves believing that His love comes without any expectations of us. But the Bible is clear that we cannot expect to receive mercy from God while denying it to others. Jesus taught this in the parable of the unforgiving servant, which He interpreted to mean that our heavenly Father will not forgive us if we don't forgive our brother (Matthew 18:21–35).

We are required to be merciful and forgive (Matthew 5:7, Luke 6:36, Colossians 3:13, Psalm 18:25). Let's seek to live our lives in agreement with James 2:13, where mercy is our reflex, not judgment.

Prayer. Make a conscious effort to pray especially for those in different political or ecclesiological streams than you. Pray for them, not against them. Pray for their families, pray for success and favour in their portfolios and churches, pray for their personal wellbeing. As we do, He will slowly disclose His heart for them to us.

This is why we at NHOP strongly recommend that all believers make a habit of praying the Word. In addition to the Lord's Prayer, the Bible is loaded with the prayers of righteous men and women. Because they're recorded for us in Scripture, we know without a shadow of a doubt that they are inspired by God Himself.

Think of it: God has literally shown us how and what to pray! When you pray the prayers of Scripture, you can be confident that you are praying in accordance with God's heart.

---

[19] Preston Sprinkle, *Does The Bible Support Same-Sex Marriage?* (Colorado Springs, CO: David C Cook, 2023), 25.

If you want to know how to pray for people, look at the apostolic prayers. There are dozens of them in the New Testament, and they're great whether you're repeating them word for word or using them as guides.

You'll notice a couple of things about these prayers: they're always directed to God, and they're always focused on releasing the good things of the Kingdom. They never emphasize shutting down what the enemy is doing.

It helps to remember that our battle is not against flesh and blood, and our weapons are not carnal (Ephesians 6:12, 2 Corinthians 10:4–6). When we perceive political or church leaders promoting agendas contrary to the Kingdom of God, we need to resist seeing them as the enemy. Remember that they are the ones Christ died for. He longs for them to be reconciled to Him.

You might be eager to point out that Paul delivered over to Satan some who stood as adversaries to the gospel (1 Timothy 1:20, 1 Corinthians 5:5), but several factors go into a move like that. Excommunication was certainly not Paul's first step. We want our default response to be in line with Jesus' primary desire to see none perish but all come to repentance. There is a time and a place for church discipline. Judging and cancelling people is often our first response, but it shouldn't be.

We also encourage people not to primarily address the enemy in prayer. First, because we don't really see that modelled in the recorded prayers of Scripture. Second, because we see greater results when we pray for the Kingdom of God to be released! Jesus came as the light of the world, and the darkness could not overcome that light (John 1:5). Our time and energy are better spent praying to the One who is light, agreeing with Him for His plans and purposes to overcome darkness in the lives of the ones we pray for. Watch what He does as you pray like that.

Embrace humility, show mercy, and pray—especially for those who think differently than you, even those who persecute you. It's essential that we move away from partiality and an us vs. them mentality, becoming aware of how God wants to draw close the very ones we once considered enemies. We must seek to be impartial.

ESSENTIAL #5

Minister to the Poor (James 2:14–26)

> ...*faith by itself, if it does not have works, is dead.*
> (James 2:17)

We now arrive at perhaps the most wrestled-over statement in the book of James: faith without works is dead. The contention dates back to the Reformation, when Martin Luther famously took issue, to some degree, with this statement. Having come from a paradigm of earning salvation through works and indulgences, Luther's eyes were opened to the simple truth that we are saved by grace through faith, that Abraham's example is about demonstrating that we are declared righteous because of our faith in God. This foundational truth sparked the Reformation, so it's kind of a big deal.

Having come from such a heavy works background, Luther was perhaps a bit triggered by James' call for good works. But that may have been James' very intention. He was writing to a collection of primarily Jewish new believers who had just come out of a heavily legalistic religion of their own.

Think back to the Gospels and Jesus' ministry. The most visible promoters of this legalism were the Pharisees, with whom Jesus had multiple run-ins. According to the Jewish historian Josephus, there were approximately six thousand Pharisees in the first century.[20] Their origins as a sect devoted to a strict interpretation of the Mosaic Law date back to at least 150 B.C. They developed a set of oral extensions

---

[20] Clayton Harrop and Charles W. Draper, "Jewish Parties in the New Testament." *Holman Illustrated Bible Dictionary* (Nashville, TN: Holman Bible Publishers, 2003).

of that law to ensure absolute obedience to the fullest degree humanly possible.[21]

The believers James wrote to had just come out of this tradition of salvation by works, just like Luther.

By swinging from a saved-by-works mentality to a saved-by-grace mentality, we can conclude that works have no place in the gospel and that the only thing that matters is whether or not we believe. This reasoning fed various forms of gnosticism in the early church, which emphasized the immaterial (soul and spirit) as all that really mattered, and the material (physical) as irrelevant or evil. This is where we get the type of thinking that says, "It doesn't matter what you do with your life as long as your heart is in the right place."

This perspective is still embraced, and even rapidly growing, in some corners of the church today. It's not too hard to find preachers who imply that you can live however you want, as long as you believe.

James' words bring balance to the relationship between grace and works in the Kingdom of God. We still need this balance today.

Some get uncomfortable when reading James 2, thinking that he's arguing our salvation is earned by our good works. He's not. There is no contradiction here with the Pauline doctrine that we are saved by grace through faith. In fact, Paul testified that he himself preached this same idea. He preached throughout Judea that everyone, Jew and Gentile alike, *"must repent of their sins and turn to God—<u>and prove they have changed by the good things they do</u>"* (Acts 26:20, NLT, emphasis added).

James and Paul both assert that good works are the evidence, the proof, of our faith. Do you see the difference? Good works are produced where the rubber of faith meets the road in our day-to-day lives.

James argues that any faith without evidence of good works is dead. He goes so far as to question whether that faith is truly a faith unto salvation (James 2:14, 17). That's a big statement!

But he backs this up with examples.

First, he points out the illogic of "just believing." All the demons in hell also believe in God, and it doesn't do them any good (James

---

[21] Bradley T. Johnson, "Pharisees," *The Lexham Bible Dictionary*, (Bellingham, WA: Lexham Press, 2016).

2:19). To the compromising believer who hides behind mere belief in God, James appears to respond with an unenthusiastic "Wow, great job." Maybe he'd add a sarcastic slow clap for good measure.

His primary example for faith with works is Abraham, the father of our faith and the very one who was declared righteous because he believed. James asks, *"Was not Abraham our father justified by works when he offered up his son Isaac on the altar?"* (James 2:21) That's a good question.

Hebrews 11:19 tells us that Abraham's faith convinced him that God could raise Isaac from the dead. That's wonderful. But how could we ever be convinced that Abraham truly believed God in this way if he hadn't followed through on that faith by being willing to offer up Isaac as a sacrifice?

You can read the story in Genesis 22. Abraham followed through on his faith. He made all the necessary preparations, went on a three-day journey (as a very old man), climbed Mount Moriah, built an altar, literally tied up his son, and laid him on a pile of wood. Yikes! Abraham didn't just tell God, "I believe You." He demonstrated his belief by obeying the command God had given him.

We know how the story ends. God intervened and provided a ram for Abraham to sacrifice instead. This is a beautiful foreshadowing of Jesus' substitutionary death in our place.

But don't miss the result of Abraham's demonstration of faith: the Angel of the Lord called out to him from the heavens and declared, *"[N]ow I know that you fear God, seeing you have not withheld your son, your only son, from me"* (Genesis 22:12, emphasis added). Abraham's actions proved the faith that was in his inner man. He had a vibrant, living faith because it came out in his actions.

James concludes his point about Abraham by saying, *"You see that a person is justified by works and not by faith alone"* (James 2:24). The word translated as justified, *dikaiouta*, carries an idea of being shown to be right.[22] Our works are the evidence of faith that has made us right with God. Note that the same point is made in 1 John 3:7.

---

[22] James Swanson, *A Dictionary of Biblical Languages: Greek New Testament* (Bellingham, WA: Logos Bible Software, 2001), #1467.

By contrast, James says that faith lacking good works is useless (James 2:20) and dead (James 2:17, 26). Faith is not genuine or alive until it's borne out in good works, influencing how we spend our time, money, and energy.

It's important to note that James makes his point about good works in the context of ministering to the poor.

Some argue that other people's mix of gifts leads them into good works, but their own has more to do with waiting on the Lord. Others emphasize focusing on the first commandment, to love the Lord your God with all your heart, because it's more important than the second commandment, to love your neighbour as yourself. The Lord might lead us through seasons of greater emphasis on certain disciplines or practices, but those are seasons, not entire lives.

I hope that through this chapter, you will see that good works are an invitation to all believers. And if you feel your primary calling is to the secret place of prayer, then know that not only is this applicable to intercessors, but it's essential to an effective prayer life.

THE IMPORTANCE OF MINISTERING TO THE POOR

The poor are consistently highlighted throughout Scripture as people God has His eye on. We can include immigrants, refugees, the diseased, outcasts, widows, and orphans in that group. As we've already seen, we are called to be as He is in the world. If we are to be extensions of Him—His hands and feet, as we often say—then our hearts need to be moved by the same things that move His. And the poor certainly move His heart.

Many, many statements in the Old Testament illuminate this point. Right from Israel's birth as a nation and the establishment of its civil laws, the people were instructed to be mindful of the poor and provide for them (Exodus 22:25–27, 23:11, Leviticus 19:9–10, 23:22, 25:35–37, Deuteronomy 14:28–29, 15:7–11, 24:12–15, 17–22, 26:12–13). On the precipice of entering the Promised Land, God commanded Israel to remember the poor, making a promise to bless them if they faithfully obeyed Him in this matter. If they neglected to do this, they would be cursed (Deuteronomy 28). Throughout Israel's history, God commonly charged His people for neglecting the poor when warning them to repent and return to Him (Isaiah 1:17, 58:7, 10, Zechariah 7:9–10).

More than just requiring this of the people of Israel, God held even Gentile nations and leaders accountable. When thinking of Sodom and Gomorrah's judgment, we can immediately pin it on their sexual immorality. Genesis 19 and Jude 7 make this very clear.

But God also made an interesting statement to Ezekiel: *"Behold, this was the guilt of your sister Sodom: she and her daughters had pride, excess of food, and prosperous ease, but did not aid the poor and needy"* (Ezekiel 16:49). Sodom's pride and excessive luxury created a *"prosperous ease"* that led them to neglect the poor and pursue carnal pleasures for themselves. Does that sound like any other culture you know of? The takeaway here is that God listed Sodom's neglect of the poor—in addition to sexual immorality—as a cause of her judgment.

In the New Testament, this emphasis continues. Jesus clearly upheld the command to minister to and care for the poor (Matthew 5:42, 19:21, 25:35–36, Luke 3:11, 6:30–35, 12:33, 14:13–14, 18:22). He extended great honour to the poor.

In Mark 12, He pointed out a widow to His disciples, using her as an example of pure worship and obedience in comparison to the rich around her.

In Luke 16, He made a poor man named Lazarus the protagonist of one of His parables. Many of His recorded miraculous healings benefited beggars and leprous social outcasts who would have been poor, as they wouldn't have been permitted to associate in the marketplace.

Jesus even personally identified with the poor by being born and raised in a poor family. We see this not only in His birth in a humble stable, but also in the story of His dedication in Luke 2. Mary and Joseph could only afford the poor man's version of the purification offering after childbirth (Leviticus 12).

From His upbringing to His teachings and actions, it's safe to say that Jesus' heart was oriented toward the poor.

This emphasis continued into the age of the apostles and the early church. The believers distributed food to the poor and widows, and as the church grew the apostles appointed seven reputable men to oversee the distribution (Acts 6:1–8). They did this so they themselves could continue focusing on the Word, prayer, and preaching.

Following these men's appointment, the signs and wonders previously done at the hands of the apostles now were done through Stephen, one of those serving the poor. Not only did Stephen start moving in signs and wonders, but his preaching brought conviction and couldn't be withstood. This powerful working of the Spirit in his life earned him the distinction of becoming the first martyr.

While the apostles focused on the Word, prayer, and preaching, Stephen stepped up to the plate and functioned in all those things while also serving the poor. His ministry is the last we read of such a great measure of signs, wonders, and apostolic preaching in the city of Jerusalem.

We also have the example of Paul. This apostolic missionary travelled from city to city with a small team. In each new place, he did the work of evangelist, church planter, teacher, and pastor, all while interceding daily for the other churches he had planted and writing various letters to admonish and encourage them.

Oh, and he did this all while working to support himself, lest he be a burden to these fledgling churches (Acts 18:3, 1 Thessalonians 2:9, 2 Thessalonians 3:8, 2 Corinthians 11:9). If anyone had a lot on his mind and plate, it was Paul.

In Galatians 2, Paul recounts the events of the Jerusalem council, first told in Acts 15, when the leaders of the church commissioned him as an apostle to the Gentiles. As they sent him out, they gave him one final instruction: *"All they asked was that we should continue to remember the poor, <u>the very thing I had been eager to do all along</u>"* (Galatians 2:10, NIV, emphasis added). With all that Paul already carried on his heart, he wasn't too busy to remember the poor.

Paul also corrected the rich among the believers in Corinth for how they had been neglecting the poor in their love feasts (1 Corinthians 11:17–34). In James 5, James also corrected the rich, and he did so with harsh language. The apostles and members of the early church clearly placed a high priority on ministering to the poor.

ESSENTIAL #5: MINISTER *to the* POOR

I would like to make one last point to this end. Jesus gave some profoundly sobering instruction regarding ministry to the poor in Matthew 25:31–46. It's sobering because it comes to us in His teaching on the final judgment, using a metaphor about sheep and goats. He very clearly describes sheep, those who will enter the eternal Kingdom of God, as those who feed the hungry, give drink to the thirsty, clothe the naked, and visit the lonely, the sick, and the imprisoned. Conversely, He categorizes the goats, those who will enter *"the eternal fire prepared for the devil and his angels"* (Matthew 25:41), as those who failed to do those same works. He is very clear that there isn't any wiggle room on this point.

Now, we know that we are saved by the grace of God, made available through Jesus' substitutionary death and resurrection, through our confession and repentance of sin, belief, and submission to God (John 14:16, Acts 4:12, Romans 3:21–30, 10:8–13, Galatians 2:16).

But don't James' statements reconcile these statements with Matthew 25? He argues that any faith that doesn't produce good works is dead and useless. He even questions whether such a faith is able to save.

Jesus didn't say we are saved by our good works, but He does appear to support James' assertion that a truly saving faith will evidence itself through good works. Vice versa, if a person's life produces no good works, do they have a saving faith?

Jesus promoted this line of thought on another occasion, too, telling the unbelieving Jews to look at His works as the proof of who He was (John 10:25).

Many discuss the Matthew 25 passage in the context of "sheep nations" and "goat nations." The Greek word translated as nations is *ethnos*, which refers to a large people group with common cultural ties. This clearly implies a large group of people of a common culture, not leaders and governments. Jesus went on to say that He *"will separate people one from another as a shepherd separates the sheep from the goats"* (Matthew 25:32). While we have already seen that God remembers how nations treat the poor, we need to also see that this passage tells us we will be evaluated on this matter individually. It is of eternal importance that we not hide our faith under a basket but display it through good works, especially to the poor.

But what does that look like, for our faith to be displayed through good works?

> If a brother or sister is poorly clothed and lacking in daily food, and one of you says to them, "Go in peace, be warmed and filled," without giving them the things needed for the body, what good is that? (James 2:15–16)

James says that it's not good enough to tell someone in need, "God bless you. I'll pray for you."

You may be thinking of another verse we seemed to pass over: *"Religion that is pure and undefiled before God the Father is this: <u>to visit orphans and widows in their affliction</u>, and to keep oneself unstained from the world"* (James 1:27, emphasis added). James tells us that we have an obligation to meet people's tangible needs whenever possible.

When word gets out about someone who lives this selflessly in North America, it creates a buzz, because it's rare. According to James, this should be the normal way of life for those of us who are in Christ.

PRAYER AND MINISTRY TO THE POOR

Okay, so you may be wondering: how is this connected to the concept of prayer? The answer really caught me off-guard. It's amazing to see what unravels when you pull on this thread. I was surprised by just how many supporting passages make the same point, that doing good works for the poor is essential for effective prayer.

Isaiah 58 is a chapter about ineffective prayer and fasting, and God's remedy to make them effective again. This chapter is a must-read for anyone who sees a life of prayer as their primary calling.

We'll paraphrase our way through the passage, but please take the time to read, pray through, and meditate on this chapter for yourself.

God sent Isaiah to the people of Israel to tell them why their prayers weren't being answered (Isaiah 58:1). They seemed to love God. They went to the temple, appeared to love learning about Him, were confident that they followed His laws, and loved being in His presence (Isaiah 58:2–3). That all sounds good, right?

But for some reason, their prayer and fasting seemed to fall on deaf ears. God told them the problem: their hearts were still far from Him. While they were going through the motions of making pious displays of humility, they still took advantage of the poor by oppressing workers and fighting and quarrelling (Isaiah 58:4). They thought God wanted to see symbolic actions of humility. But God was looking for true humility in their actions toward employees and one another.

We are not justified by external religious works alone, especially when they don't sync with the state of our hearts. When we try to become righteous by doing religious things, it's merely self-righteousness. This cannot make us clean (Isaiah 64:6). We have to get our hearts right first. Good works flow from that. This is what Jesus meant when He said, *"First clean the inside of the cup and the plate, that the outside also may be clean"* (Matthew 23:26). The real test of whether we have truly rent our hearts in humility is demonstrated in how we relate to others, especially those we think are beneath us.

When we try to get God to answer our prayers by doing the right religious things, like prayer and fasting, while remaining unchanged in our hearts, it's not at all pleasing. He sees through it, and it stinks. Perhaps the harshest expression of that reality comes to us from Amos:

> I *hate*, I *despise* your feasts, and *I take no delight* in your solemn assemblies. Even though you offer me your burnt offerings and grain offerings, I will not accept them; and the peace offerings of your fattened animals, I will not look upon them. Take away from me the noise of your songs; to the melody of your harps I will not listen. *But let justice roll down like waters, and righteousness like an ever-flowing stream.* (Amos 5:21–24, emphasis added)

Those are strong words! Isaiah said the same thing, but more gently: the fast that really gets God's attention includes extending justice to victims of injustice, lightening the burdens of those you employ, setting the oppressed free, feeding the hungry, providing shelter for the homeless, clothing the naked, and helping relatives who need it (Isaiah 58:6–7).

A few verses later, God highlights a few more things He looks for. We must stop putting oppressive burdens on, pointing fingers at, and speaking viciously to others. Instead we need to pour ourselves out for the hungry and help those in need (Isaiah 58:9–10). Everything He's looking for is essentially wrapped up in the command to love your neighbour as yourself.

God then promises to respond to the prayers of those who demonstrate good works to the poor. Look at the list of His promised answers to those who embrace good works:

> Then shall your light break forth like the dawn, and your healing shall spring up speedily; your righteousness shall go before you; the glory of the Lord shall be your rear guard. Then you shall call, and the Lord will answer; you shall cry, and he will say, 'Here I am.' If you take away the yoke from your midst, the pointing of the finger, and speaking wickedness, if you pour yourself out for the hungry and satisfy the desire of the afflicted, then shall your light rise in the darkness and your gloom be as the noonday. And the Lord will guide you continually and satisfy your desire in scorched places and make your bones strong; and you shall be like a watered garden, like a spring of water, whose waters do not fail. And your ancient ruins shall be rebuilt; you shall raise up the foundations of many generations; you shall be called the repairer of the breach, the restorer of streets to dwell in. (Isaiah 58:8–12)

What a list! Is there a better description of victorious Kingdom living than that? And it all hinges on prayer and fasting *coupled with* extending good works to the poor and needy.

Here are a few more passages demonstrating this connection between answered prayer and doing good works for the poor:

> The eyes of the Lord watch over those who do right, and his ears are open to their prayers. But the Lord turns his face against those who do evil. (1 Peter 3:12, NLT)[23]

> Blessed is the one who considers the poor! In the day of trouble the Lord delivers him… (Psalm 41:1)

> Whoever closes his ear to the cry of the poor will himself call out and not be answered. (Proverbs 21:13)

> "As I called [for them to show kindness, mercy, and justice], and they would not hear, so they called, and I would not hear," says the Lord of hosts… (Zechariah 7:13)

Those final two passages are difficult to read but incredibly clear: if we close our ears to the cries of the poor, He will close His ears to our cries. Wow!

This is an example of the command that says, *"Freely you have received; freely give"* (Matthew 10:8, NIV). If we want to receive mercy, we must extend mercy. If we want to receive forgiveness, we must extend forgiveness. If we want God to listen to our cries for help and answer our prayers, we must listen and respond to the cries for help of those around us. The link is inescapable.

Prayer, fasting, worship, and all the other spiritual disciplines are good. We certainly should not ignore them or throw them out. But just

---

[23] This passage quotes Psalm 34:15–16. Note the contrast between *"those who do right"* and *"those who do evil."* This clearly implies that the righteous are those who do what is right. In other words, their faith is expressed in good works.

as James argues that a faith lacking good works is dead, a prayer life that is unaccompanied by good works to the poor and needy is ineffective.

Similarly, Jesus rebuked the scribes and Pharisees for spending their attention on tithing proper amounts of mint and cumin while neglecting the weightier matters of the law: justice, mercy, and faithfulness (Matthew 23:23). He didn't tell them to respond by rejecting tithing, but to add works of justice, mercy, and faithfulness to their tithes.

We know that God is attracted to the humble and lowly, raising up the ones who have been brought low (1 Samuel 2:8, Isaiah 61:1, 66:2, Psalm 12:5, 34:18, 35:10, 51:17, 72:12, 112:9). It stands to reason that if we want to see God at work among us, we should associate with the poor and lowly.

The story of Cornelius provides a surprising and wonderful example of this. Acts 10 marks a pivotal shift in the storyline of the Bible. Having been hinted at for years, this is when God finally throws open the doors of the Kingdom to the Gentiles, welcoming whosoever would believe in Him.

Cornelius, a Roman centurion, sent for Peter and his team to visit his home. Comforted by an open vision he received immediately before this invitation, Peter went to Cornelius' home and testified to the ministry, death, and resurrection of Jesus. The Holy Spirit then fell on everyone present, baffling Peter and his friends and creating a huge stir in the church that took years to sort through.

Indeed, it is still being sorted through today.

So how did God choose who would be the first fruits of this Gentile harvest? He didn't pick a family at random. He was drawn to Cornelius' household for a reason: *"At Caesarea there was a man named Cornelius… a devout man who <u>feared God with all his household, gave alms generously to the people, and prayed continually to God</u>"* (Acts 10:1–2, emphasis added).

Notice the three things listed together: Cornelius feared God, gave generously to the poor, and prayed continually. We know that the centurion's giving was important because of the angel's follow-up declaration: *"Your prayers and your alms have ascended as a memorial before God"* (Acts 10:4).

ESSENTIAL #5: MINISTER *to the* POOR

Cornelius wasn't chosen because he prayed faithfully. He was chosen because he was as diligent in giving to the poor as he was in praying faithfully. Both actions, done in the fear of the Lord, ascended before God as a memorial.

We often think of our worship and prayer as sweet-smelling incense rising before God. How often do we think of acts of mercy and justice to the poor as having the same effect? According to this account, they do.

Because of this combination of continuous prayer and generous almsgiving in the fear of the Lord, Cornelius' household became the epicentre of the Holy Spirit's explosion into the Gentile world.

Think of all the revivals that have happened among Gentiles through church history, and that are still happening today. They all started with Cornelius. It's likely that most people reading this book are, in fact, Gentiles. In some measure, we owe thanks for our inclusion in the Kingdom of God to this Roman centurion's lifestyle of prayer and almsgiving.

MOVING FORWARD

I hope you are convinced by now of the powerful role of generosity to the poor in increasing the effectiveness of your prayer life. If this is something you've been involved with in the past, that's awesome. Keep it up! If not, my heart is not to guilt-trip anyone, since condemnation does nothing helpful. But if you've been stirred even a little bit, please let that compel you to action.

I would say this: start small. Don't set unrealistic targets for yourself. You're likely not going to solve all the issues of poverty in your city in the next year or two. That's okay. He's looking for a "yes" in your heart, a willingness to respond to what the Holy Spirit is showing you. Ask Him to begin opening your eyes to the poor, lonely, marginalized, and outcast.

One of the sad realities today is that these communities are steadily growing. Homelessness is on the rise. Mental health awareness is at an all-time high, yet the associated stigma still makes it difficult for many to make inroads. Cancel culture pressures us to write off everyone who messes up, but even the imprisoned need visitors. We are surrounded by invitations to respond to this call. We just need to have the same response Isaiah had when his eyes were opened: *"Here am I! Send me"* (Isaiah 6:8).

Start small, responding to the invitations He gives you. Do it in wisdom. Partner with a church or ministry in your city that's already doing this. Invite brothers and sisters to join you.

It may feel a bit overwhelming and you may not know where to start. I think God would give us the same encouragement He gave to the exiles tasked with rebuilding the temple: don't despise the day of small beginnings (Zechariah 4:10). Just start where you can, being faithful in the small things, and if He sees fit He'll lead you into more. Be faithful. Sign up for what you can do consistently. Be a faithful, consistent presence where you can.

I acknowledge that it's much more comfortable to stay in our prayer closets. There's less unknown, less mess. But He is with the poor, outcast, and oppressed, and He beckons us to join Him. When we get with them, we find ourselves in His line of sight, too.

We would often rather attract and invite the upper middle class, but that's often not where the most fruitful harvests are found (1 Corinthians 1:26). Conversely, James says that God has chosen those who are poor to be rich in faith and heirs of the Kingdom (James 2:5). Do we want to be among those who are more likely to enter the Kingdom with gratitude and a huge "yes" in their spirits, or among those who ridicule the Name by which we are called (James 2:6–7)?

Our desire is to see the church in Canada awaken to her calling to preach good news to the poor, that she wouldn't leave it to the government to care for them but instead step in to be the hands, feet, and pocketbook of Jesus. In so doing, we believe with confidence from the Word that we will see a tremendous shift in the effectiveness of our prayers.

Again, the Word is very clear: if we ignore the cries of the poor, He will ignore our cries.

ESSENTIAL #6

Freshwater Speech (James 3:1–12)

> *...blessing and cursing come pouring out of the same mouth... this is not right!*
> (James 3:10, NLT)

As we move into James 3, I want to acknowledge that this is the passage that really opened up our journey into the book of James. It makes sense to share the origin story behind how we got here. Not surprisingly, it all started in a prayer meeting.

Throughout the COVID-19 pandemic, NHOP had to pivot in how we functioned. We couldn't invite people to come to Ottawa to pray, as most travel was strongly discouraged. Even if people could come to Ottawa, we couldn't gather in person to pray together.

Like most people, we got acquainted with Zoom. Instead of drawing people to Ottawa to pray, we connected with Canadians across the country to pray together for Ottawa and the rest of our nation. We know we weren't the only ones doing this: many online prayer initiatives started or grew during this time. It's been so exciting to see these prayers mobilized across the country, not only in that season but on an ongoing basis!

In our little stream, we give a fair bit of attention to praying for government and the news and events around it. The trick is, as we discussed earlier, to avoid the constant supply of opportunities to become anxious, upset, or offended at the happenings in government. It can be difficult to track with the political sphere and not get caught up in negativity. It's important work to do, because those feelings can very easily leak out in our prayers.

On one of our weekly prayer calls, around September 2021, someone prayed straight out of James 3:9–12, praying that the church in Canada would no longer speak both blessing and cursing out of the same mouth, whether praying for or speaking about our leaders.

This really resonated with us on the call. There was something to it.

The passage kept coming up, week after week. We continued praying along these lines, for God to speak to the church and give her grace to clean up her speech, especially concerning elected leaders. We knew God was breathing on this prayer.

As confident as we were about that, it locked in for us through a testimony. One of our dear friends and prayer team members, Pam from Manitoba, shared something with us a month later. She had purposed in her heart to take this passage seriously, to the point of removing herself from conversations when people started to complain about or slander the government. She didn't quietly slip away but made sure her friends knew that she was leaving out of a choice to intentionally bless and not curse with her mouth. She did this with believing and non-believing friends alike.

As a result, she noticed a definite shift in how she prayed for our government, and a greater sense of peace, answers to prayer, the nearness of God, and His leading.

That may not sound like much. You may have heard more exciting testimonies. But this was big to us. When we carry a burden around in prayer that only leaves us fearful, anxious, and stressed out, we're missing something.

Jesus told us that His yoke is easy and His burden is light. This doesn't mean that everything will be easy. We know that we'll face difficulties and that it won't be comfortable to daily take up our cross and follow Him. But He did promise to be with us, and that peace and joy can be ours in any situation (Matthew 28:20, John 16:33, Romans 14:17, Philippians 4:6–7, 11–13). If we finish our prayer times feeling stressed, anxious, or even angry, we may be carrying the wrong burden, or carrying it with the wrong yoke.

Pam's testimony of seeing a noticeable increase in peace and joy as she prayed for our government, confirmed to us that there was something to this. As James wrote, we only experience the intended blessing when we do what the Word says.

We are confident that the nature and tone of the words we use when praying for or talking about people are significant. This isn't surprising when we consider what Scripture has to say about the weight of our words.

THE WEIGHT OF OUR WORDS

It's difficult to miss the forcefulness of James 3:1–8. He leaves no room for doubt as to what he believes about the tongue, and his words should inject sobriety in how we understand its power. Just look at some of these statements:

- If you can control your tongue, you are a perfect (complete) man (James 3:2).
- The tongue is as influential to us as a little rudder is to a ship (James 3:4).
- The tongue is *"a whole world of wickedness"* (NLT), able to corrupt the whole body (James 3:6).
- Our tongue can put us in danger of being sent to hell (James 3:6).
- You are more likely to tame every type of creature than your tongue (James 3:7).
- The tongue is restless, evil, and full of deadly poison (James 3:8).

These are strong words! Dwell on them long enough and you might consider taking a vow of silence. This passage can make controlling the tongue seem like a nearly impossible task.

Thankfully, nothing is impossible with God.

Solomon identified the influence of our words very plainly when he said, *"Death and life are in the power of the tongue…"* (Proverbs 18:21) With our words we can curse, cut down, and destroy; or we can build up, encourage, and comfort. The more we use our tongues, the more we reap the fruit of what our words produce.

It's somewhat interesting to note the arrangement of these words, with "death" being highlighted before "life." Perhaps this is meant to instill some caution as we choose our words!

What makes our tongues so weighty, with the potential to be so dangerous? It seems that the first indication of this appears back in Genesis 1:26. We have been made in the likeness of the God, who created the cosmos by the word of His mouth.

Numerous scriptures paint a picture of the power released when God speaks (Genesis 1, Job 26:14, Psalm 29, Matthew 17:5–6, 21:18–22, Luke 24:32, John 11:42–44, Revelation 1:15). This doesn't mean our words carry the same power as His words; we cannot create worlds with a word, just as we cannot do the works Jesus did out of our own strength.

I'm not parroting the New Age thinking that suggests we can manifest what we want by simply speaking it into existence, nor am I supporting a name-it-and-claim-it brand of faith. As explored earlier in this book, our words are most effective and powerful when they are in line with His, when we say what the Father is already saying… you know, like Jesus did.

But this one thing is certain: our words are not meaningless.

Part of the dignity of being human is the fact that God is always mindful of us (Psalm 8:4–8, 40:17, 139:1–6, 17–18, 144:3). We haven't been created and subsequently ignored.

Part of His awareness of us includes our speech. He knows the words we speak, remembers them, and relates to us according to them (Psalm 139:4, 50:14–15, 61:5, Ecclesiastes 5:4–5, Malachi 1:14). He acts as though we mean what we say.

This is consistent with His character as the covenant-keeping God, as demonstrated throughout Israel's history. The nation of Israel voluntarily confirmed the Mosaic covenant with God (Exodus 19:8), and throughout the rest of the Old Testament we see the people experience blessings and curses as they fulfilled or broke the terms of that covenant. They spoke and agreed to the terms of the covenant, and God related to them by those very words.

ESSENTIAL #6: FRESHWATER SPEECH

A thought-provoking example of the effect of our words is seen in Genesis 27, when Jacob deceived Isaac to steal Esau's blessing. While Esau was out hunting, Rebekah prepared a meal just the way Isaac liked it and sent Jacob in to see him with the food. Jacob dressed himself in Esau's clothes and draped goat skins on his arms to mimic his older brother's hairiness. Isaac thought something was up but went ahead and pronounced a blessing over the one he thought was his favourite son.

When Esau came later with his prepared meal, we read that Isaac trembled with anger at the discovery that Jacob had deceived him. His reaction tells us that he was furious and regretted blessing Jacob. He clearly would have taken it back if he could.

But note what he says to Esau: *"Who was it then that hunted game and brought it to me, and I ate it all before you came, and I have blessed him? Yes, and he shall be blessed"* (Genesis 27:33, emphasis added). Though Isaac was tricked and pronounced the blessing unwittingly, what he had said could not be undone. Even though Esau begged with bitter tears, Isaac could do little for him. He had pronounced the blessing and couldn't take it back, though the circumstances seemed unfair.

That's a very sobering thought.

Another example would be a story we referenced earlier, where the people of Israel made a treaty with the Gibeonites in Joshua 9. Though the Gibeonites were among the people that the Israelites were supposed to drive out of the land, this covenant later had to be honoured. This led Israel into what must have seemed like a disastrous situation. In Joshua 10, we read that five Canaanite kings joined forces to attack Gibeon, forcing Israel to come to the defence of their new allies.

Taking on five armies at once likely produced some fear. But an incredible thing happened: God gave Israel the victory, even causing the sun to stand still in the sky for a full day so Israel could chase down every last one of their enemies. This miraculous victory happened precisely because Israel had kept their word, even when it looked like it would cost them dearly.

Psalm 15:4 tells us that God has a soft spot for people who keep their word even when it hurts.

On the flip side, God remembered and held Israel to the terms of this covenant centuries later. In 2 Samuel 21, Israel experienced three years of famine during David's reign because Saul had ignored the treaty with the Gibeonites, putting many of them to death. God held Israel accountable to their words.

Because God takes our words seriously, we ought to be continually mindful of what we say. It's a great privilege and honour to know that the God of the universe cares about what we say and puts such great stock in our words. But there is a great responsibility in this as well. Many passages exhort us to use our speech for the purpose of producing life and not death.

Here are just a few examples from Paul's epistles:

> Let no corrupting talk come out of your mouths, but only such as is good for building up… (Ephesians 4:29)

> Let there be no filthiness nor foolish talk nor crude joking… instead let there be thanksgiving. (Ephesians 5:4)

> Let your speech always be gracious, seasoned with salt… (Colossians 4:6)

> But avoid irreverent babble, for it will lead people into more and more ungodliness, and their talk will spread like gangrene. (2 Timothy 2:16–17)

Jesus addresses our speech in the Sermon on the Mount. There we find one of the simplest and clearest commands concerning our words: *"Let what you say be simply 'Yes' or 'No'; anything more than this comes from evil"* (Matthew 5:37).

Would you be surprised to know that James quotes this statement in James 5:12? This instruction is a call to integrity in our speech. We are to mean what we say and say what we mean, to follow through on our words.

ESSENTIAL #6: FRESHWATER SPEECH

As Proverbs 18:21 implies, the more we talk, the more we run the risk of saying something that produces consequences. Half-truths and outright lies can easily hide in a multitude of words; loopholes are created where words carry on. But a simple, straightforward yes or no doesn't leave room to hide. This kind of speech is comfortable in the light, with nothing hiding in the shadows. That's where we want to be.

This is about more than just thinking carefully about what we're going to say before we say it. Our speech is the overflow of what's inside, revealing what's going on in our inner man. When rebuking the Pharisees for carelessly blaspheming the Holy Spirit in Matthew 12, Jesus said,

> You brood of vipers! How can you speak good, when you are evil? *For out of the abundance of the heart the mouth speaks.* The good person out of his good treasure brings forth good, and the evil person out of his evil treasure brings forth evil. I tell you, on the day of judgment *people will give account for every careless word they speak,* for by your words you will be justified, and by your words you will be condemned. (Matthew 12:34–37, emphasis added)

This means that our words reveal what's in our hearts. Even the most careful, meticulous crafters of speech won't be able to stop the real fruit from making its way out at some point. Our speech is among the fruits from the tree of our lives and it has a way of revealing whether we're healthy trees or diseased (Matthew 7:15–20).

Let's go back to our text. In James 3:9, he states that some believers make a practice of blessing our Lord and Father but then cursing people out of the same mouth. We sing songs of praise in the congregation, extolling God for being beautiful, gracious, loving, and good, and we may even make a habit of proclaiming His goodness to friends and neighbours who don't yet know Him. But then, with that same mouth, we'll deal in grumbling, gossip, and assumptive accusations about people who were made in the image of the same God we've recently magnified.

From the same mouth proceed blessings and curses, which are inconsistent with each other. Hopefully you see something wrong with that!

James brilliantly uses examples from nature to make his point: *"Does a spring pour forth from the same opening both fresh and salt water? Can a fig tree, my brothers, bear olives, or a grapevine produce figs?"* (James 3:11–12) Everyone knows that you can't drink the water from the Pacific Ocean, or that you won't find saltwater in the Great Lakes. Have you ever picked a fig from a grapevine? Of course not. Grapevines produce grapes, fig trees produce figs, and freshwater springs produce freshwater. That's simply a law of nature.

It's not natural for a grapevine to produce two different types of fruit. Neither is it natural for the mouth of a believer to speak both blessings and curses, life and death. This leads us to a difficult but necessary question: does the spring of my mouth naturally produce freshwater, or saltwater? And if we don't like the answer to that question, how do we change it?

BECOMING A FRESHWATER SPRING

Another passage of Scripture touches on fresh and salt water. Can you think of where it is? It's a little bit surprising, and it beautifully complements James 3.

The final nine chapters of Ezekiel feature a magnificent vision he had of a restored temple in Jerusalem. He had been in exile for twenty-five years and Jerusalem itself had been utterly destroyed fourteen years prior.

The Lord took Ezekiel to Jerusalem and showed him this new temple in remarkable detail. After seven chapters of thoroughly detailing the rooms and dimensions of this temple, Ezekiel was taken outside to see something else: a bit of water exiting the temple toward the east. The wording makes it sound like it wasn't an impressive flow, just a trickle (Ezekiel 47:1–2).

The angel didn't allow Ezekiel to ignore this trickle and move on. The angel followed the water, measuring off one thousand cubits (roughly five hundred metres). At that point, he led Ezekiel into the water, where the trickle had developed into an ankle-deep stream.

The angel then took Ezekiel the same distance further, where the water was knee-deep.

After another identical length, the water was waist deep.

He measured off another thousand cubits, and Ezekiel said that the river had grown too deep to stand in; it was sink or swim.

Here's where things get interesting. When Ezekiel was led back to the shore of the river, he noticed that the banks flourished with trees. The angel explained that everywhere this river went, it brought vibrant life.

Why is that interesting? Because if you consider the geography around Jerusalem and the path this river took, it was emptying into the Dead Sea.

The Dead Sea has the distinction of being the lowest body of water by elevation on earth.[24] Water flows in, with all its minerals and other solids, and has nowhere to go. The water evaporates in the Middle Eastern heat, leaving the mineral content behind. It's one of the saltiest bodies of water on earth, so dense that swimmers can float on the surface with virtually no effort. And because of the high salinity, there is no aquatic life in the Dead Sea and its banks are barren.

The Dead Sea is a perfect example of what we know happens in the natural: when freshwater and saltwater collide, the saltwater always wins out. The freshwater becomes salty. It never works the other way around.

Yet here we see an absolute miracle: this river, flowing from the temple in Jerusalem, arrives in the Dead Sea and makes it come to life.

The angel explained the purpose of the river to Ezekiel: *"For this water goes there, that the waters of the sea may become fresh; so everything will live where the river goes"* (Ezekiel 47:9). This river brings the life of God to dead places.

Consider two of the results. The first is abundant fishing, which Jesus used as a metaphor for evangelism in calling Peter and Andrew

---

[24] Kenneth Pletcher, "The Dead Sea," *Encyclopedia Britannica*. October 25, 2022 (www.britannica.com/place/Dead-Sea).

to follow Him. The second is an abundance of trees on either side of the river, all of which produce fruit year-round. The river is cited as the reason for this fruitfulness, and the fruit these trees produce is intended for food and healing.

This passage is echoed in Revelation 22:2, where the river of the water of life is described as flowing out from the throne, watering trees that produce leaves for the healing of the nations. The passage is often quoted in reference to the prophetic significance of the maple leaf on Canada's flag.

But what does this mean for us on a personal level? In John 7, Jesus showed up in Jerusalem during the feast of tabernacles. On the last day of the feast, Jesus stood up in the assembly and cried out, *"If anyone thirsts, let him come to me and drink. Whoever believes in me, as the Scripture has said, 'Out of his heart will flow rivers of living water'"* (John 7:37–38). Jesus was clearly referencing the same Ezekiel 47 river we just looked at.

Lest there be any confusion, John adds some commentary for us in the passage: *"When he said 'living water', he was speaking of the Spirit..."* (John 7:39, NLT) This river, which brings life to dead places and turns saltwater into freshwater, speaks of the person and work of the Holy Spirit.

If you're born again with the Spirit of the living God dwelling in you, this transformation is yours. It's one aspect of the new creation we have become (2 Corinthians 5:17).

One of the Holy Spirit's tasks is to bring the life of God into the dead areas of our lives, making them come to life. Sometimes we allow an area of sin to continue influencing us. The process of considering ourselves dead to those things and allowing His new life to find expression in us is the process of sanctification (Romans 6:1–14).

Allowing the freshwater of that internal river of life to find expression in our speech is one of the ways in which we are sanctified and become more like Him in this world. The good news is that He will help us make the change! We must do our part to spend time in the river and be willing to relinquish the saltwater and allow Him to bring up the freshwater.

ESSENTIAL #6: FRESHWATER SPEECH

PRAYING FOR OUR NATION AND THOSE IN AUTHORITY

Over the past few years, as political divides have deepened, we've heard many people pray for the removal of leaders and governments. Is this not cursing those very leaders? Jesus refers to the accuser as the thief whose only aims are to steal, kill, and destroy (John 10:9). When we pray for a leader to be impeached or imprisoned, for their term to be cut short—or worse yet, for personal harm to come to them (and yes, we've heard those prayers)—are we not agreeing with the destroyer?

What about unrighteous laws that clearly advance the cause of death and destruction of the family? What about legislation that clearly encroaches on long-enjoyed freedoms of conscience, belief, religion, and speech? It can feel like every couple of months another precedent seems to move us toward the Bible being declared hate speech and Christianity being outlawed. Shouldn't we be angry about that? Shouldn't we oppose and push back?

Even if we were to find ourselves in a place of state-sponsored persecution, as the early church did, here are an assortment of instructions for how we should respond:

> But I say, love your enemies! Pray for those who persecute you! (Matthew 5:44, NLT)

> But to you who are willing to listen, I say, love your enemies! Do good to those who hate you. Bless those who curse you. Pray for those who hurt you. (Luke 6:27–28, NLT)

> Bless those who persecute you; *bless and do not curse them*... Beloved, never avenge yourselves, but leave it to the wrath of God... Do not be overcome by evil, but overcome evil with good. (Romans 12:14, 19, 21, emphasis added)

When reviled, we bless; when persecuted, we endure…
(1 Corinthians 4:12)

If you need a refresher, go back to Essential #3 for a review. We don't have a green light to curse when we're anxious or upset. That might look like complaining with family or friends, or sharing memes and cartoons that insult people on social media. Yes, James 3 also applies to our social media habits.

Remember, we don't wrestle against flesh and blood, so we shouldn't direct our weapons of warfare against others. The example presented to us throughout the New Testament is one of praying for the release of the blessings of the Kingdom of God, not against the works of the enemy.

Let's take a look at one example of this in practice from the early church.

In Acts 3, Peter and John made their way to the temple for a time of prayer, and on their way they encountered a lame beggar. They healed him in the name of Jesus, which stirred up a huge commotion. This was a notable miracle, since everyone who frequented the temple knew this beggar. The miracle opened the door for Peter and John to boldly declare the gospel.

However, the religious leaders quickly descended on them with an order to cease and desist, forcing them to leave the temple grounds. The leaders threatened them against preaching Jesus in the future (Acts 4:21).

How did Peter and John respond? They called a prayer meeting! In this time of prayer, those assembled quoted Psalm 2: *"Why did the Gentiles rage, and the peoples plot in vain? The kings of the earth set themselves, and the rulers were gathered together, against the Lord and against his Anointed"* (Acts 4:25–26).

Does this not feel like an applicable passage for us today? There is a growing rage against the Lord and His ways, a concerted effort to change laws and sway culture from the boundaries God has laid out for us, in favour of the right and freedom to do whatever feels good. It is the regression of Romans 1 and we're watching it unfold at an ever-quickening pace before our eyes. So maybe there's something for us to learn here.

ESSENTIAL #6: FRESHWATER SPEECH

Back to Peter, John, and their fellow believers. How did they respond to the threat of this coordinated rebellion?

> And now, Lord, look upon their threats and grant to your servants to continue to speak your word with all boldness, while you stretch out your hand to heal, and signs and wonders are performed through the name of your holy servant Jesus. (Acts 4:29–30)

Notice two things in this prayer.

First, they didn't pray for the political situation to change. They didn't pray for the gag order to be overturned so they could preach in peace and safety. No, they prayed for grace to continue preaching with boldness in the face of opposition. They didn't pray for the leaders to back down or be removed, but they prayed for grace that they themselves might not back down. They didn't try to control the leaders; they prayed for power to stay faithful to what God had commissioned them to do.

As explored earlier, many times our prayers to see a government toppled are rooted in our own fears, and those fears are usually related to a potential change to our sense of what's normal. We quickly conclude that judgments are the right way to pray for a government that's walking away from Him. Yes, there is a time for judgment of wickedness. But again, we don't want to rush into that. Amos warned, *"Woe to you who desire the day of the Lord [judgment]! Why would you have the day of the Lord? It is darkness, and not light…"* (Amos 5:18–19) It's like Amos was saying, "You don't know what you're asking for when you pray for judgment."

Peter warned that when judgment comes, it touches God's household first (1 Peter 4:17). We should be aware that if judgment were to fall on Canada, it would only come after God had dealt with the dross in the church first. Thank God He is longsuffering for mankind's sake, giving ample time for all to repent (2 Peter 3:9).

As a rule, we should pray for the welfare of the places we live. That was the instruction Jeremiah gave the exiles (Jeremiah 29). They were aliens in a foreign land, just like we are as citizens of the Kingdom of heaven here on the earth. Our hearts should be to see our nation and its leaders walk in the peace, prosperity, and welfare of God. We call people to repentance and reconciliation with God as a ministry of restoration (Matthew 3:2, Mark 9:12–13, 2 Corinthians 5:18–20) so it will go well for our land.

There is a time when God moves in judgment, but His desire is to show mercy (James 2:13, Micah 7:18). We ought to embody the same priorities in our hearts, speech, and prayer.

The second point about the prayer in Acts 4 is that they prayed for God to show up. They didn't pray for the work of the enemy to stop or fail, but for the Kingdom of Light to show up in power and overwhelm the darkness with healing, signs, and wonders performed in the name of Jesus.

Paul took a similar approach when he entered Corinth for the first time. He didn't attempt to win the people with reason or polished speeches, but they came to the knowledge of God by the demonstration of the Spirit and of power (1 Corinthians 2:1–5).

It's interesting to consider that Paul, before heading to Corinth, spent time in Athens.[25] While there, he did some excellent apologetics work, but the result was a mixed bag of mocking, tickled ears, and a few conversions (Acts 17:32–34).

When he left Athens for Corinth, he was determined *"to know nothing among [them] except Jesus Christ and him crucified"* (1 Corinthians 2:2) and to see demonstrations of the Spirit in power.

In carnal and intellectual Greece, which bears many similarities to our own culture today, demonstrations of the power of the Spirit appear to have proven more effective than persuasive preaching alone. Our prayer similarly needs to be for the Kingdom to show up in power.

So here is the encouragement: give more attention and energy to blessing than cursing. Set your heart on seeing the Kingdom of Light expand. This may seem overly simplistic, but it's true. The best way to get rid of darkness is not to try to remove darkness, but to turn a light on.

---

[25] You can read about this journey in Acts 17:16–34.

When our eyes are fixed on what's happening around us, it can feel like we're in a losing battle. But that's not at all a reflection of reality. He came as the Light and the darkness could not overcome Him (John 1:5). Scripture is loaded with assurances of Christ's total victory and the promise that it will be shared with those who endure to the end (Psalm 2, 110, Isaiah 2:1–4, Daniel 2:44, 7:13–14, 22, 27, Romans 16:20, Revelation 11:15).

We don't have to live from a fear of Christ and His church losing. We need to remember that we are seated with Christ in heavenly places (Ephesians 2:6) and receive His invitation to *"come up here"* (Revelation 4:1), knowing that we will be able to see from His eternal perspective when we slow down, rest, and listen to Him. Sometimes it takes a little work to enter that rest, but it's worth it.

It's important to acknowledge that David prayed many times for God to destroy his enemies (Psalm 10:15, 58:6–9, 59:11–13, 69:22–28, 109:6–20) and that Jeremiah's prophetic ministry was at least partially *"to pluck up and to break down, to destroy and to overthrow"* (Jeremiah 1:10).

We aren't wrong to cry out for justice. In fact, we're commanded to! But in the New Testament, we are also told to set our hearts to repay evil with good (Matthew 5:43–48, Romans 12:18–21). As discussed in Essential #2, if ever we are to pronounce some sort of judgment, it must be initiated by the Father. He alone judges with perfect righteousness and equity. We are not to pray or speak in these ways any time we feel like it, which can be often. We must learn to discern between our feelings and the leading of the Lord. Err on the side of blessing.

Scripture tells us that a city can be exalted by the blessing of the upright, or it can be overthrown by the mouth of the wicked (Proverbs 11:11). So we pray for the release of blessing. Pray for the word of the Lord, the good news of the Kingdom, to run swiftly and be glorified, directing hearts into the revelation of His love for them. Pray that He would demonstrate His total victory over sin and death through healing. Pray that He would demonstrate His omniscience and lovingkindness to those who don't know Him, through the prophetic gift at work in His people. Pray that Canadians, including those in positions of authority, would taste and see that He is good. Pray that the Lord of the harvest would send forth labourers into the harvest (2 Thessalonians 3:1, 5, 1 Corinthians 14:24–25, Psalm 34:8, Luke 10:2). Pray the text of Joel 2:28–32, that what He began in the upper room on the day of Pentecost would continue and be fulfilled, leading to the gospel of the Kingdom being proclaimed throughout the world as a testimony to all nations. Pray that His church would become the pure, spotless, radiant bride He will return for. Pray for the day of His appearing (Revelation 19:7–8, 22:17)!

Learn to bless with your prayers, but also let your speech match your prayer. We must speak with integrity. We cannot pray to God for blessing, then curse men to other men. Pray for those who persecute you. Bless those who curse and misuse you. When reviled, bless instead. Let your speech always be gracious, as though seasoned with salt. May we be as He is in this world, the One who was full of grace and truth, anointed with the oil of gladness and whose speech dripped with grace (John 1:14, Psalm 45:2, 7).

I challenge you to commit yourself to speaking life and blessing, and to refrain from sinning by cursing others (Job 31:30, Proverbs 14:21). As the old adage reminds us, "If you can't say anything nice, don't say anything at all." As small as it seems, refrain from sharing that insulting meme or piling on with another joke. I'm confident that you'll notice a change for the better in how you see the ones you used to speak ill of, and you'll see a change in your prayer life.

EVIDENCE THAT THIS WORKS

We'll close this chapter with one more testimony.[26]

Louise is a friend of NHOP from central Canada. She joins our prayer calls when her work schedule allows and tracks with our Canopy of Prayer initiative.[27] She works as a nurse. During the COVID-19 pandemic, she quietly wrestled with her conscience over whether she should get the vaccine. She decided not to get it.

---

[26] I've changed the names in this story at our friend's request.
[27] See Appendix B.

ESSENTIAL #6: FRESHWATER SPEECH

Now please don't get hung up on issues related to the pandemic or the vaccine, whichever side of the argument you fall on. It's not the main point here; I only mention it to help set the context.

In Louise's region, the vaccine was not mandatory for health workers, so she was able to keep working. One day she overheard a group of nurses having a conversation about the pandemic and the vaccine. She overheard one of her friends—we'll call her Joanne—exclaim that she wished all unvaccinated people would just die, as it would solve everybody else's problems.

This was obviously incredibly difficult for Louise to hear, and her heart's first response was anger. But she said that the Lord reminded her about the charge to love our enemies and pray for those who persecute us. God asked her, "When is the last time you prayed for Joanne?" So instead of confronting Joanne in anger, Louise began to pray for her.

Months later, a miracle occurred. A patient of Louise's required life-saving surgery. In the weeks leading up to the surgery, Louise and many others prayed diligently for this patient.

When the time came for surgery, the doctors opened her up and found everything to be normal. There was no evidence of what all the tests had pointed to.

Word spread in the hospital, and a group of nurses, including Joanne, asked Louise what had happened. Louise told them that they'd laugh at her if she answered honestly, but they persisted. Louise relented and told them the only explanation: it was a miracle. She had been praying, and many of this patient's friends and family had been praying. The nurses were stunned and quiet. According to Louise, the room felt tense.

Now, that healing is a miraculous testimony in and of itself! But the fun part is that it was setting the stage for another testimony of God's goodness.

Later, Joanne pulled Louise aside and asked if she would pray for her. Louise *wanted* to say, "Well, if you had your way, I'd be dead right now and that would be impossible."

Thankfully, she held her tongue!

Joanne went on to tell her that she and her husband had been having trouble conceiving for a long time and were getting desperate. Louise told her that she would pray, and she invited a few prayer groups to agree with her in prayer. Louise had one condition before God: "Only do this if she knows it was because You intervened."

As life went on, Louise checked in every month or so to see how Joanne was doing, ask if there was any news, and offer words of encouragement.

One day, Louise had an opportunity to lay hands on Joanne and pray for her in the hospital. The moment was so divinely orchestrated that it caught Louise's attention, and she took note of the date.

A couple of months later, Louise received a video call from Joanne. This was odd to Louise because they had never communicated by this method in the past.

When Louise answered the call, she saw that Joanne was crying… and holding a positive pregnancy test! Joanne explained that she knew it was a miracle from God because she had stopped seeking medical intervention.

"I know this happened because you prayed, and because of God," Joanne said.

When Joanne revealed the due date, Louise did the backwards math and made an exciting discovery: the conception had likely happened the day she'd laid hands on Joanne and prayed for her.

Months later, Louise worked up the courage to tell Joanne about the whole "I wish you were dead" thing. It turns out that while Joanne had been part of that group conversation, she hadn't been the one who made that statement; she herself had been unsure of her stance. It turned out that Louise had gotten the source wrong.

But that doesn't change the point of this testimony. Louise had been reviled. Despite getting the details wrong, she still faced a choice: fight fire with fire or choose to bless. As far as Louise knew, Joanne had spoken a death wish over her, and she had responded by praying for new life in Joanne.

Realize that if Louise had spoken harshly to Joanne from her hurt, the only likely results would have been a fight, a broken relationship, and a hostile work environment. Even when discovering the case of mistaken identity, Joanne likely still would have been offended by the hostile accusation. That door would have been shut and locked.

Because Louise bit her tongue and chose to bless instead of curse, Joanne is now tasting and seeing the goodness of God firsthand in her life. A testimony of the goodness and power of God is growing in a family that hadn't previously known Him or walked with Him.

In more ways than one, life is winning over death!

Let this testimony be a reminder that freshwater speech—a commitment to bless even when everything in our flesh wants to curse—paves the way for God to move and demonstrate what He's like.

Louise's anger would not have produced the righteousness God intended for this situation; in fact, it would have short-circuited His plans. Sure, God could have found another way to work this miracle in Joanne's life, but Louise would have missed out on the joy of partnering with God in it.

When we set our hearts on blessing and peacemaking, we reflect His character in our world.

In the Sermon on the Mount, Jesus calls peacemakers sons of God and equates loving our enemies with being perfect as our heavenly Father is perfect (Matthew 5:9, 48). When we pray from a heart that reflects Jesus' heart, we pray in His name—and Jesus said that He answers those prayers because they glorify the Father (John 14:13).

Beloved, I implore you: use your tongue to bless and not curse! Your prayer life will flourish as you do.

ESSENTIAL #7

Heavenly Wisdom (James 3:13–18)

...the wisdom from above is...
willing to yield...
(James 3:17)

Up to this point, James has addressed several topics that concern our actions and therefore are quantifiable. For one, we are to be quick to listen, slow to anger, and impartial. For a second, our faith is played out in good works. Thirdly, we are to choose blessing over cursing. I say these topics are quantifiable because we can look back over a period of days, months, or years and measure whether we've changed or grown in these areas. It's something we can track.

We've also seen how Scripture details the impact these various behaviours have on the effectiveness of our prayers. For example, it's easy to draw a straight line between "minister to the poor" and "effective prayer."

In these latter chapters, James shifts from quantifiable behaviours to beneath-the-surface heart issues. We could think of them as the roots that produce some of the fruits we've looked at. Being internal, these are a little more difficult to measure. It's the stuff only you and the Holy Spirit can truly see.

These final passages feature two closely related themes that keep jumping off the page to me: humility and meekness. No matter how hard we try, we can't get around them, so we might as well explore them.

TWO WISDOMS

James progresses from the power of our words and how we use them to talking about wisdom. This is a look at the underlying, motivating factors behind our words. Whether our words are like a freshwater or saltwater pond, the wisdom that governs our heart is like the spring that supplies that pond. Or if we see our words as fruit from the tree of our life, the wisdom to which we subscribe is the root system that feeds that fruit, making it either healthy or diseased.

Wisdom is a bit like the wind, in that it can't be seen or quantified except by its effects in the lives of people who live by it. The right wisdom produces good fruit, such as being quick to listen, slow to speak, slow to anger, impartial, and so on.

The contrast between wisdom from above and earthly wisdom is consistently shown throughout the New Testament. Paul writes that the wisdom from above is not of this age. It doesn't agree with natural human thinking and can seem downright foolish to the carnal mind. It only makes sense to those who have received the Spirit of God (1 Corinthians 2:5–7, 14).

Jesus illustrates the same point in Luke 18:15–17 when He declares that the Kingdom of God belongs to the ones who come to Him with childlike faith, as opposed to our human wisdom and knowledge. The wisdom of man is foolishness to God, and His foolishness is wiser than anything humanity's best thinkers could come up with (1 Corinthians 1:18–31). Again, His ways are not our ways and His thoughts are much higher than our thoughts (Isaiah 55:8–9).

James shares his own take on the matter, offering several contrasts between these opposing wisdoms. An entire book could be written to unpack these, but we will look at just two of them here.

The first point of contrast between these two wisdoms is related to our speech.

James says that the one who is wise and understanding should show his works in the meekness of wisdom (James 3:13). By contrast, James warns the ones motivated by an earthly wisdom to not boast and be false to the truth (James 3:14).

ESSENTIAL #7: HEAVENLY WISDOM

Do you see the difference? The wisdom from above is more concerned about demonstrating itself through good works, being seen and not heard, while earthly wisdom is connected to deception and boasting, which carries the idea of slick, deceptive, or perhaps even brash talk.

In Proverbs, wisdom is consistently connected with silence or measured speech, while foolishness is paired with an unrestrained tongue (Proverbs 10:19, 12:18, 13:3, 15:4, 16:23, 27, 17:27–28, 18:6, 21:23, 22:11, 29:11).

This wisdom comes to us from an ancient eastern culture, yet we still recognize it to be true in Western culture today: those of few words are generally regarded as wise. Still, carnal wisdom urges us into arguments and debates, seeking to win people over by forceful and persuasive words (boasting), and perhaps a gentle massaging of the truth (deception) when necessary. This may relate to our culture's craving for immediacy; maybe with one debate we can get everything sorted out, right?

Jesus touched on this idea of silent wisdom in a discussion about John the Baptist (Luke 7, Matthew 11). He spoke of John's ministry and lifestyle, even declaring him to be the greatest man ever born of a woman (Luke 7:28). That's high praise, coming from the Son of God!

Then Jesus turned to the Pharisees and lawyers to address a hypocrisy of theirs. They had labelled John a demoniac because of his extreme fasting, but they had also labelled Jesus a glutton and drunkard because He didn't fast, joining in feasts with tax collectors and sinners (Luke 7:33–34). So they criticized John for fasting too much and Jesus for not fasting enough. They jumped to conclusions and then hurriedly aired their opinions to the listening crowds.

But Jesus called them out for their hypocrisy, finishing with a peculiar statement: *"Yet wisdom is justified by all her children"* (Luke 7:35). Matthew records the same statement in his account, but he uses the word "deeds" in place of "children" (Matthew 11:19).

Matthew's account echoes what James says of our faith: wisdom is justified by her deeds, by her works. The word that Jesus used is a variation on the same word James uses—*"You see that a person is justified by works and not by faith alone"* (James 2:24)—so they were kind of making the same point: wisdom is not proven by talk. You have to wait to see the works, the deeds, the fruit that is produced over time. The works show the nature of the wisdom, whether it's good or bad, heavenly or earthly. In a sense, Jesus was saying, "I'm not going to argue with these guys. Just look at the fruits of their lives, then look at the fruit of My life and the fruit of John's life. Who would you rather follow?"

This is one of wisdom's stumbling blocks to us today: it takes time.

Again, Luke used the word children in place of deeds. Children take time. Lots of time. Nine months of gestation, and that's only the beginning. You're looking at another twenty years or so before those children are mature and able to stand on their own. That's twenty years of nurturing, teaching, training, growing, playing, correcting, maturing, and testing. After all that, we don't really know what the fruit of their lives will be until they move out and build lives of their own. Though we do see hints of their root system as they grow and mature, we don't see the fruit until they get out from under the shade of their parents' tree and become their own. Twenty years!

The same principle is seen with actual fruit. From the day they're planted, most fruit trees won't bear any meaningful fruit for three to ten years. That's at least three years of nurturing, pruning, and waiting until you see confirmation of what kind of fruit tree you have, and whether it's healthy or diseased. They just take time. There's no way around it.

You can't convince someone of wisdom in a debate. It's only proven over the course of a lifetime. Wisdom isn't justified (shown to be right) in words, but in the works it produces. This is why James argues that it's crucial for our faith to be demonstrated by good works, which are what demonstrate the wisdom of the gospel, the culture of the Kingdom, and the power of God in our lives. The wisdom from above is proven by her children, good deeds, and not by words.

Remember, Paul understood this. As we've already seen, this understanding shaped his approach in reaching the carnal city of Corinth with the gospel. His debating and apologetics in Athens hadn't produced the kind of fruit he was used to seeing, so as he continued to Corinth he resolved to put his wisdom in the backseat and instead emphasized the crucified Christ and demonstrations of the Spirit and of power (1 Corinthians 2:1–5).

ESSENTIAL #7: HEAVENLY WISDOM

Again, the wisdom of God isn't proven so much in debates as in good works.

The second point of contrast for James is the nature of the fruits produced by these two types of wisdom. Notice the clear dichotomy between the terms used in James 3:14–17 to describe earthly and heavenly wisdom:

Earthly Wisdom	Heavenly Wisdom
Bitter jealousy	Peace
Selfish ambition	Willing to yield
Boasting	Gentleness
Vile	Pure
Lying and deception	Sincerity
Disorderly	Bears good fruit

James portrays earthly wisdom as self-promotion that justifies any means to achieve its ends. It's loud, brash, deceitful, and willing to create a bit of chaos for the sake of getting ahead. Selfish ambition is rooted in comparison, trying to get ahead of others. That type of thinking always produces striving and anxiety.

His description of heavenly wisdom, on the other hand, presents no evidence of striving. It's peaceful, gentle, sincere, genuine, and doesn't need to prove anything. It keeps bearing good fruit no matter what's going on around it. It's a picture of rest in the midst of anxiety.

In a word, the wisdom from above is meek (James 3:13). You will only find it among the humble (Proverbs 11:2).

WISDOM IS WILLING TO YIELD

Of all its characteristics, I think meekness is what really sets heavenly wisdom apart. The trouble is that meekness can be downright offensive to our carnal thinking. One of the Greek words James used to describe this wisdom is *eupeithes*, which means "easily persuaded."[28] This word

---
[28] Swanson, *A Dictionary of Bible Languages: Greek New Testament*, #2340.

gets translated several different ways: submissive, compliant, reasonable, open to reason, and willing to yield.

Compliant? Submissive? Willing to yield? These descriptors are hardly held in high regard today. Who would be honoured to be labelled as compliant or submissive? Those who are compliant and submissive are sometimes mockingly referred to as sheep. But doesn't the Bible refer to us as sheep…?

First, it's important for us to rightly understand the concept of meekness. To the world, meekness is synonymous with weakness. Someone who's meek is a pushover, unable to defend or stand up for themselves. Have you ever heard the world talk about meekness in a positive light?

But the meekness Jesus embodies, and calls us to, is very different. True meekness is power under restraint. Jesus walked the earth as the omnipotent God, but He voluntarily restrained all that power and submitted to the will of His Father. Think about it: He could have emptied every grave during His earthly ministry, but He didn't. He could have transfigured Himself before every resident of Judea and Galilee, but He didn't. As mentioned earlier, He only did what He saw the Father doing.

Some of the greatest passages that illustrate Jesus' meekness include Isaiah's prophecy about Jesus (Isaiah 42:1–4), Jesus' submission of His will in the garden of Gethsemane (Matthew 26), and the great declaration of His humility (Philippians 2:5–11).

Meekness is the result when one has the power to do something but chooses not to. It is self-controlled. Again, it is power under restraint. This was the meekness of Jesus. He could have appealed to the Father and been delivered by twelve legions of angels (Matthew 26:53), but He voluntarily endured the cross. No one took His life, but He laid it down.

On the other side of the ledger, carnal wisdom argues that if you're right—and wisdom is always right, isn't it?—then you should fight to win every discussion, argument, or debate. You should be the strongest and most persistent voice. Wisdom should be the last one standing, every time. It needs to have the last word and come out on top. Right? Doesn't the one who yields in a debate admit defeat? How will anyone see the truth if wisdom doesn't win the argument?

ESSENTIAL #7: HEAVENLY WISDOM

The problem is that diligence, persuasion, and even aggression in the arena of debate has no bearing on whether the point being argued is true. There is a well-known adage that has long been attributed to the Nazi minister of propaganda, Joseph Goebbels. He is believed to have said, "If you tell a lie big enough and keep repeating it, people will eventually come to believe it." More than a saying, researchers have successfully demonstrated that people are more likely to believe repeated information than new information, regardless of whether the information is true or false. They call it the illusory truth effect.[29]

This basically means that we tend to believe what we hear repeated the most. This is concerning given the stream of opinion and information constantly bombarding us through smartphones, computers, and TVs.

We can logically conclude that diligent, persuasive, or forceful speech isn't sufficient to prove wisdom. If anything, this human tendency to trust the loudest, more persistent message can be manipulated; we call that propaganda. It has also been said that if someone can talk you into something, then someone else can talk you out of it.

So, you see, wisdom is not proven in the arena of debate, even though that makes the most sense according to our thinking.

Jesus, on the other hand, was a master of unresolved conversations. He frequently answered questions with a question of His own, sidestepped questions altogether, or even floated questions and walked away without waiting to see if His listeners got the right answer.

One such example comes from the Passion Week, in one of Jesus' final public discourses. In Matthew 21:23–27, the chief priests and elders demanded that Jesus tell them who gave Him the authority to preach and perform miracles. Jesus responded by telling them that if they could figure out where John the Baptist got his authority from, they'd have their answer. Seeing that they were trapped, the religious leaders responded by saying, "We don't know." Jesus was content to leave them in that state, moving along in the discourse without giving them an answer.

---

[29] Aumyo Hassan and Sarah J. Barber, "The Effects of Repetition Frequency on the Illusory Truth Effect." *Cognitive Research: Principles and Implications, 6(38)*. May 13, 2021 (www.ncbi.nlm.nih.gov/pmc/articles/PMC8116821).

Jesus had put a question to them that would lead them to the truth. When they were unwilling to follow it, He left them in their unbelief. He didn't try to persuade them or win the debate with an impressive one-liner and mic drop. He was secure enough in the truth to leave the question hanging and walk away.

Heavenly wisdom is not bent on winning arguments. It plays the long game, confident that it will be proven right in due time. It's more concerned with winning hearts than winning arguments.

We see this in Jesus' instructions for dealing with interpersonal relationships and confrontations: *"If your brother sins against you, go and tell him your fault..."* (Matthew 18:15) The natural, or carnal, reading of this statement leads us to think, "I'm supposed to go to my brother and tell him exactly what he did to me and how he hurt me. He needs to know that he's in the wrong and I'm right." We are often motivated to make that person feel our anguish, driven by a desire for vengeance or retribution. We want to be proven justified in our offence.

But notice the motivation Jesus says we are to have in all this: *"If he listens to you, you have gained your brother"* (Matthew 18:15, emphasis added).

The goal is not to win the argument, be proven right, or be declared a legitimate victim deserving of retribution. The goal is a restored relationship, to win your brother back. There are obvious limits and boundaries to this; Jesus goes on to say that if your brother is unrepentant, certain consequences must take effect (Matthew 18:15–17). He wasn't creating a mechanism to keep people in abusive relationships or shield wrongdoers from accountability, as some have twisted it to say. Nevertheless, He makes it plain that the whole purpose of the exercise is to restore relationship if at all possible, not vent an offence and prove one party right over the other.

Each of these examples demonstrates something of meekness, a willingness to yield. Not needing to have the last word, to let a conversation go unfinished, is a form of yielding. To lay down your right to be offended and instead offer forgiveness is another form of yielding. This willingness to yield is something we're all called to walk in, and it's more than a suggestion. James argues that we are required to do this by law. It's the law of liberty.

THE LAW OF LIBERTY

James twice refers to this law of liberty (James 1:23–27, 2:12–13). In the first mention, he uses the phrase to describe the perfect law, or the whole of Scripture. This is done in the context of looking into the Word as someone looks into a mirror, persevering until they begin to live out what they see there. As they do what they read, they are blessed in their doing.

In the next sentence, James lists the resultant good deeds: bridling the tongue, visiting lonely orphans and widows, and leading a holy life. Restrained speech, serving others (good works), and walking blamelessly are fruits of the law of liberty, and of heavenly wisdom.

His second mention comes in the context of addressing the sin of partiality. In that passage, he first mentions that the royal law is the standard by which we should live: love your neighbour as yourself (James 2:8). This is a great time to remember the parable of the good Samaritan. The term neighbour in this context essentially refers to anyone, and specifically people we don't like.

When we don't love our neighbour, James says that we're committing the sin of partiality. Further, he says that if we sin in one point against the law, we transgress the whole law. We are as guilty of violating the law as a murderer or adulterer, even if we haven't done those things ourselves (James 2:9–11).

That's a tough pill to swallow. What are we to do with that?

> So speak and so act as those who are to be judged under the law of liberty. For judgment is without mercy to one who has shown no mercy. Mercy triumphs over judgment. (James 2:12–13)

This is interesting wording, because the law of liberty we are judged under actually sets us free. At the cross, Jesus paid every debt of sin for all who are in Him, and our result is freedom. James is saying, "Remember that you've been forgiven on account of the mercy of God. If God has been merciful to you, you must be merciful to others." In other words, living with the understanding that we're set free under the law of liberty should produce a merciful disposition in us toward others. A merciful disposition looks a lot like meekness.

Paul writes about the same principle in Romans 13–14 and 1 Corinthians 8–9. It's very interesting that both conversations happen around food.

A little bit of context would be helpful here.

One of the challenges facing the early church was how to graft Gentiles in with the Jewish believers to become the body of Christ. The question was essentially, "How Jewish do these Gentile believers need to become?" They wrestled over customs such as circumcision, ceremonial food laws, and other questions related to the Mosaic law. This struggle built to a climax at the Jerusalem council of Acts 15, where the apostles and elders debated whether the Gentiles needed to be circumcised and keep the whole law of Moses in order to become part of the church.

After vigorous debate, it was concluded that only four burdens should be laid on Gentile converts: abstinence from food sacrificed to idols, from eating blood, from eating what had been strangled, and from sexual immorality (Acts 15:29). Eating meat that had been sacrificed to idols was too closely connected to the worship of idols, so that was prohibited. Eating blood or meat from an animal that had been strangled and not properly drained infringed upon the command to refrain from eating blood, which represents the life of a creature.

In a sense, these four guidelines comprised a command to worship God alone, acknowledge the sanctity of life, and abstain from sexual immorality.

As far as the food laws went, this conclusion was a sort of common ground for Jew and Gentile. Gentiles were asked to follow minimal Jewish expectations in these regards, and the Jews were to accept their Gentile brothers without demanding they become as strict as the Jews themselves.³⁰ We can conclude that at least part of the goal was to get these Jewish and Gentile believers to find some common ground and grow in unity.

Guess what? The struggle didn't miraculously end there. It continued to be a point of contention. Paul was dogged by Judaizers who sought to convince recent Gentile converts that they still needed to be circumcised and adhere to the law of Moses. We see clear evidence of this battle in Paul's letter to the Galatians.

In Rome, believers faced this dilemma with an interesting variable at play. During the reign of Emperor Claudius, all the Jews were expelled from Rome.³¹ Many believe this happened around 49 A.D. The city, and thus the church in that city, essentially became one hundred percent Gentile overnight. These Gentile believers were suddenly free from having to appease their Jewish brothers' consciences around food. Naturally, they would have become very comfortable in their rhythms as a church body without all those so-called legalistic demands.

This continued for about five years until Emperor Claudius died, the edict ended, and the Jews could return.

Imagine the resulting situation. The Gentile believers had gathered for five years, eating whatever they were comfortable with at their love feasts, and suddenly the Jewish believers and their ceremonial food laws were back.

The Gentile brothers weren't so eager to relinquish the liberty they'd enjoyed. In fact, the Gentiles' cold reception of their Jewish brothers led to some measure of discord in that church.

Paul addresses this throughout the letter of Romans. He spends the first few chapters emphasizing that both Jew and Gentile are in need of the righteousness of God, which only comes through faith. He then spends three chapters (Romans 9–11) detailing the relationship between Gentile and Jewish believers, emphasizing that the Gentiles shouldn't be arrogant toward their Jewish brothers, nor be ignorant of their continued standing as the covenantal people of God.

---

[30] Craig S. Keener, *The IVP Bible Background Commentary, Second Edition* (Downers Grove, IL: InterVarsity Press, 2014).

[31] Arnaldo Dante Momigliano, "Claudius: Roman Emperor," *Encyclopedia Britannica*. May 29, 2024 (https://www.britannica.com/biography/Claudius-Roman-emperor).

Finally, he addresses food, a particular point of contention (Romans 13:8–15:7). It's a large passage with many excellent points, but it can be summarized in these three verses:

> So let's stop condemning each other. *Decide instead to live in such a way that you will not cause another believer to stumble and fall…*
> And if another believer is distressed by what you eat, you are not acting in love if you eat it. Don't let your eating ruin someone for whom Christ died…
> It is better not to eat meat or drink wine or do anything else if it might cause another believer to stumble. (Romans 14:13, 15, 21, NLT, emphasis added)

In the similar passage of 1 Corinthians 8–9, Paul says it this way:

> But take care that this right of yours does not somehow become a stumbling block to the weak… if food makes my brother stumble, I will never eat meat, lest I make my brother stumble. (1 Corinthians 8:9, 13)

He goes on to list several privileges he would be perfectly justified in enjoying but chose to set aside for the sake of reaching as many people as possible.

To the Galatians, he put it this way: *"For you were called to freedom, brothers. Only <u>do not use your freedom as an opportunity for the flesh, but through love serve one another</u>"* (Galatians 5:13, emphasis added). Not only is the willingness to yield a mark of heavenly wisdom, but it's also a mark of love (1 Corinthians 13:5).

We have been set free, but not so that we can do whatever we want. This was Jesus' example to us. Being sinless, He was completely free when He came to earth. Yet He submitted His will to the Father's, for our benefit. In the same way, we are invited to lay down our own privileges and rights for the sake of serving one another.

ESSENTIAL #7: HEAVENLY WISDOM

If anyone ever had the right to seek their own pleasure or gain, it was Jesus. He is the second person of the Trinity. He could have demanded to be feted, overthrown governments, performed signs and wonders publicly for financial gain, or done any number of self-promoting things. But He didn't. Instead He gave up His divine privileges, restricted Himself to a human frame, served us instead of demanding to be served, and ultimately submitted Himself to a criminal's death (Philippians 2:6–8, Mark 10:45). And He has invited us to deny ourselves, take up our own cross, and follow in His footsteps (Luke 9:23).

As an aside, it's worth noting that He leads each of us a little differently, according to how He has fashioned us. One may have a completely clear conscience regarding drinking alcohol in moderation, while another has a clear invitation from the Lord to abstain from it. Neither is more holy than the other; both have an obligation to walk with a clear conscience before the Lord and not judge the other. Concerning sin, yes, we call each other up into holiness. But we must learn to do so without judgment.

Think back to the day you were saved. Did God reveal every bad habit, every wrong motive, every wrong belief to you? Did He require you to fix everything in that first week? Month? Year? Has He not revealed more weaknesses and shortcomings as you've continued to walk with Him? Could it be that He's leading others the same way? Maybe the thing He highlighted for you on day one is something he will highlight to another in year ten.

This doesn't mean we turn a blind eye to sin. It just means that we encourage and call one another up into holiness without judgment or criticism. In other words, we do it gently.

We extend mercy because we have received mercy. Jesus came in the fullness of truth, but He somehow spoke that truth with words that dripped with grace (John 1:14, Psalm 45:2). We need to have a sober understanding of the devastating consequences of sin and deal ruthlessly with it, but we also need to restore a stumbling brother or sister in a spirit of gentleness, recognizing that our flesh is just as weak as theirs (Galatians 6:1).

The law of liberty that James speaks of demands that we deal mercifully, gently, with one another. We don't use our liberty recklessly; we voluntarily use it to serve and prefer one another. We are willing to yield. This is heavenly wisdom.

HEAVENLY WISDOM IN THE AGE OF COVID

I'll start this section with a little trigger warning. As we all remember, the COVID pandemic stirred up all sorts of anxieties. This section may bring back some of those memories. I'm not wading into any of the debates surrounding restrictions and whatnot. That is not my lane. I only hope to show how a little bit of heavenly wisdom could have helped us all navigate that season better. So please try to stick with me.

The COVID-19 virus burst on the scene in the early months of 2020, making people seriously ill, taking many lives, and rapidly spreading around the world. Because it was new, nobody could declare with any certainty how it truly behaved, how it was transmitted, how easily it was transmitted, or how to properly safeguard from it. It felt like the whole world was groping in the darkness for answers as the number of cases continued to rise.

With governments grappling over how to handle this pandemic, many unprecedented measures were adopted. In Canada, this included orders to isolate at home, and when in public to practice social distancing and wear a mask. As vaccines became available, the government strongly encouraged all citizens to get their shots, even going so far as to make vaccination a condition of employment for government positions and denying unemployment benefits to those who had lost their jobs because they chose not to be vaccinated.

These measures produced a wide range of responses. Many citizens enthusiastically embraced the government's suggestions and pleaded with others to do the same. On the other hand, many questioned the government's motives behind each restriction. Some flatly refused to comply, to the point of publicly resisting and encouraging others to follow suit. A new federal political party even formed from this groundswell of opposition.

Most Canadians landed somewhere between these two extremes.

Not surprisingly, the groups on opposite ends of the spectrum were the loudest throughout the debate. Those in favour of the restrictions vocally supported mandates, in some cases urging the government to adopt even stronger measures to encourage citizens to get their shots. They accused the sceptical and hesitant of believing and peddling misinformation. Perhaps most notably, our prime minister made remarks that painted resisters and the vaccine hesitant as second-class citizens.

At the same time, some sceptics blatantly disregarded public health measures and strolled unmasked through grocery stores and other public spaces, sometimes even intimidating people by getting face to face with the masked and taunting them. They contended that people were buying into fake news and believing government propaganda. Families, churches, and communities experienced seismic divisions as both sides dug in.

Are you starting to see where I'm going with this?

All of this came to a head in the winter of 2022, when thousands of truckers and supporters convoyed to Ottawa. There, Canadians gathered from across the country to protest perceived government overreach, which drew the ire of residents of downtown Ottawa, most media outlets, and many throughout the country at large. It escalated to the point that the federal government invoked the Emergencies Act, intended for use in times of war, in order to forcefully end the demonstration.

In just under two years, we went from dealing with a new virus to watching our government enact wartime measures to deal with protesting citizens. How did things get so out of hand?

In the months following, some people continued to display messages related to that protest on their vehicles. I saw one drive through my hometown emblazoned with this statement: "My freedoms don't end where your fears begin."

This message struck me and got me thinking. According to Jesus and Paul, your fears are pretty much *exactly* where my freedoms end, if not sooner.

A free nation can only remain free as long as its citizens respect and protect the freedoms of others. "It's a free country" isn't a good reason for someone to drive on the wrong side of the road, erect a twenty-foot fence around their property, or take something from a store because they want it. There are boundaries to freedom. You can drive almost anywhere in the country, so long as you respect others' rights to drive safely. You can build a nice fence around your property, so long as it complies with bylaws that protect your neighbour's right to a reasonable view. Laws must get stricter when selfish people violate the freedoms of others.

If this is expected of a civil society, how much more should we think like this in the body of Christ?

The wisdom from above compels us to be willing to yield to one another. In Paul's words, *"We who are strong must be considerate of those who are sensitive about things like [approved foods]. We must not just please ourselves"* (Romans 15:1, NLT).

A major cause of the escalation of tensions in Canada during the pandemic was rooted in both sides' determination to flaunt their convictions. Some who were sceptical of masks, vaccines, and other guidelines went out of their way to taunt those who were genuinely fearful of contracting the virus. Was it necessary for some of these people to cough, shout, or laugh in the faces of complete strangers who may have had compromised immune systems, or had loved ones with elevated health risks? Many shouted for freedom of conscience rights. But what about the people whose consciences led them to take precautions?

What about the other side of the debate? Some pro-restriction people celebrated the adoption of vaccine mandates, which cost fellow Canadians their businesses, careers, savings, pensions, homes, and more. These people's Charter freedoms were revoked. Polarization led many to believe that the vaccine-hesitant were all delusional conspiracy theorists. But what about those who had a genuine check in their spirit about the vaccine, no matter how much material they read about its safety and efficacy?

The truth is that the Bible says nothing about vaccines or masks. In the church world, both sides made cases for their arguments from the Bible, but there is no plain answer in Scripture on this debate. In fact, godly men and women who have walked with and loved the Lord faithfully for years came down on either side. Some believed that the

Lord invited them to pass on the vaccine, and others had complete peace about getting vaccinated. There is no definitive, one-size-fits-all, thus-saith-the-Lord conclusion to be reached on this issue.

If Paul were to speak into the situation today, what would he say? Judging from passages like Romans 14 and 1 Corinthians 8–9, I'm confident that he would tell us to make our decision from a clear conscience, and not to judge others. We should bear with one another and not make our conscience's decision a stumbling block for somebody else.

Have you ever read Jesus' thoughts about stumbling blocks? You really don't want to become one (Matthew 16:23, 18:6–9, Luke 17:1–2).

This was one of those debates where it would have been better if we had all been willing to yield to one another.

This doesn't mean we have to adopt another person's conviction at the cost of violating our own conscience. It does mean we must resist a tribalistic us vs. them mentality that looks for opportunities to draw battlelines. Again, if it's not a clear issue of sin, we need to do our best to honour and maintain relationship with those whose conscience leads them to a different conclusion. I can make room for them to follow their conscience, just as I expect them to make room for me to follow mine.

This idea of yielding has application within the life of the church as well. Literally thousands of differing denominations of belief proliferate around the globe, each with their own practices. In many cases these differences are hotly contested, with both sides declaring that they stand for truth. Of course, it's imperative for us to be faithful to the truth, but Jesus also prayed for a church that would be *"perfectly one"* (John 17:23), as inseparable as the relationship between the Father and Son.

While we must hold to truth, we must also find a way to contend for the unity of the church and not be so willing to sacrifice relationships with other parts of the body. In Ephesians 4, Paul calls for the same traits as James: humility and gentleness, along with patience.

Let's major on the majors, minor (yield) on the minors, and be humble enough to recognize when we've got them confused. As the old axiom goes, "In essentials, unity; in non-essentials, liberty; in all things, charity." There are beautiful people who truly love Jesus in all sorts of different streams, and our lives would be seriously enriched if we could learn to walk in unity with them.

The point is that we must live with a clear conscience before God. But if a brother's conscience leads him to a different conclusion on matters that aren't clear in Scripture, we are to bear with him. Be willing to yield. Prioritize the relationship. Paul's conscience was clear that all food was suitable for eating, yet he volunteered to never eat meat again if he knew it violated the conscience of a brother (1 Corinthians 8:13).

This is what it means not to use our freedom as an opportunity for the flesh. Our freedom is not a license to do whatever we want. In our freedom, we have power, by grace, to lay aside our own preferences in the name of benefitting others.

MEEKNESS PICKS ITS BATTLES

When do we stand and fight? Is there a time for that? The militant "army of God" paradigm is very popular in the Western church. But sometimes that militancy finds expression in places it maybe wasn't intended to.

Going back to the messaging on that truck, there is a common perception, even in the church, that we need to fight for our rights. But if Scripture calls us to anything, it's to deny ourselves, take up our cross, and follow Him. That is essentially a call to forsake our rights.

The only right of a cross-bearing criminal was to die. Everyone knew what the cross meant. If you saw someone carrying a cross in first-century Rome, you knew they were about to die on it. As hard as this call is, it's not unfair. Didn't He give up His rights and lay down His life for us before inviting us to do the same in return?

On the surface, this invitation makes no sense to our natural reasoning. That's heavenly wisdom for you. But we must remember that the story doesn't end there. Those who deny their flesh and remain faithful to the end will share in His resurrection and be glorified with Him forever. That glorification will dwarf the pain of sufferings experienced on earth. Paul went so far as to say they *"are not worth comparing with the glory that is to be revealed in us"* (Romans 8:18).

ESSENTIAL #7: HEAVENLY WISDOM

Instead of constantly fighting for our rights and privileges, we can invite God to be our Avenger. But He can't do that if we keep insisting on avenging ourselves.

In the life of David, we see a brilliant example of entrusting our vindication to God.

David had a significant prophetic promise over his life. He had been anointed to one day succeed Saul as the king of Israel (1 Samuel 16). In the years following, David found himself serving the man he was to succeed. He became Saul's personal armourbearer, privately ministered to him through music to soothe him when he was tormented by a spirit, and was a successful commander in Saul's army (1 Samuel 16:21, 23, 18:30). He even became Saul's son-in-law!

As far as we can see, David served Saul with excellence and integrity. Even so, Saul's jealousy drove him to seek David's life, to the extent that he even commissioned three thousand of Israel's finest warriors to hunt and eliminate David (1 Samuel 24:2).

To this point in the story, we have no indication that David had done anything to deserve this. There is no record of him sinning against God or man to bring about this season of hardship. He had done everything right. He didn't deserve this treatment!

David twice had a golden opportunity to avenge himself. The first opportunity is seen in 1 Samuel 24. While on the hunt for David, Saul retreated into a cave alone to relieve himself, not knowing that David and all his men were hiding in the recesses of that same cave. David's men urged him to act, saying, "Look! Here's the fulfillment of that prophetic word! Slit his throat and become king!" But David refused.

The second opportunity came two chapters later (1 Samuel 26). David snuck into Saul's camp in the middle of the night as everyone slept. Again, the man accompanying David encouraged him to seize his destiny by killing Saul—and again David refused.

In both instances, David got a safe distance away and then called out to Saul, imploring him to call off the assassination order, having proved that he wasn't out to harm Saul. David wasn't out to avenge himself but rather to entrust judgment of the situation to the God who sees all and deals justly with every man (1 Samuel 24:12, 26:23–

24). David would not avenge himself, because he had chosen to give that right to God.

Many years later, decades into his reign, David had a similar response in a similar situation. In 2 Samuel 15–17, his son Absalom staged a coup and stole the kingdom from him. Yet again, David didn't attack his accuser to defend himself or fight for his rights. Even when a worthless nobody cursed him as he fled Jerusalem, he wouldn't allow his men to kill the scoffer.

Twice in this story, David made statements similar to the ones he had made all those years earlier: *"It may be that the Lord will look on the wrong done to me, and that the Lord will repay me with good…"* (2 Samuel 16:12)

David is a clear and powerful example of what it looks like to refuse to be swept up in the exchange of evil for evil but to instead choose to overcome evil with good (Romans 12:21). David refused to descend into the mud pit with his opponents, opting to occupy the high ground and invite God to judge the situation.

When we fight for our own rights, we essentially tell God, "It's okay. I've got this." The problem is that we don't see all that God sees, and we don't possess perfect, bias-free judgment. We may get some revenge, and possibly even see some results, but it will never be the best resolution. In fact, we easily end up in sin ourselves. Remember what James said: *"the anger of man does not produce the righteousness of God"* (James 1:20).

When we take our hands off the situation and allow God to judge, we will reach one of two conclusions.

By entrusting judgment to God and taking the posture of blessing and praying for our enemies, the Holy Spirit can come in and do His work of convicting them of sin and righteousness (John 16:8).

The ideal situation is that the offender responds to the conviction of the Holy Spirit and receives full forgiveness for their sins, receiving the same mercy we have received. In this case, the full penalty for their sin is paid for in Jesus' atoning sacrifice on the cross.

But if they reject His overtures, they will receive the full reward for their sin on the day of judgment.

In both instances, justice is satisfied.

Even though we may be the offended one, the spotlight shines back on us. Which solution do we hope to see? Is our earnest prayer for the other person to respond to the Holy Spirit with repentance and receive full forgiveness, being reconciled back to God and us? Or, like Jonah, do we secretly hope that they never respond so we can rejoice, or maybe gloat, in seeing them receive the fruit of their sin?

How we respond to offence and wrongdoing reveals something significant about our own hearts.

If Jesus, the only sinless One, can forgive those who wronged Him, we certainly ought to forgive those who have wronged us. Overcoming doesn't look like fighting for our rights. In the upside-down Kingdom, we overcome by not loving our own lives unto death (Revelation 12:11). When we fight back in defence of our rights and privileges, we seek to avenge ourselves and refuse to entrust vengeance to the Lord.

There is, however, a time for us to stand and speak out. This happens in defence of those who cannot defend themselves, the very ones our flesh tends to overlook and brush aside (James 2:1–7). These are the ones we can stand and fight for.

Note some of these passages:

> Open your mouth for the mute, for the rights of all who are destitute. Open your mouth, judge righteously, defend the rights of the poor and needy. (Proverbs 31:8–9)

> May he [Solomon] defend the cause of the poor of the people, give deliverance to the children of the needy, and crush the oppressor! (Psalm 72:4)

> …learn to do good; seek justice, correct oppression; bring justice to the fatherless, plead the widow's cause. (Isaiah 1:17)

> Do justice and righteousness, and deliver from the hand of the oppressor him who has been robbed. (Jeremiah 22:3)

Instead of raising our voices and getting worked up about our own rights, the Bible wants us to spend ourselves on behalf of those whose voices are ignored. That seems to be the sort of situation when we are to stand up and demand justice.

If you're looking for something to take a stand for, take a stand in defence of people who are being mistreated: the poor and homeless, the unborn, the mentally ill, the refugees, or mistreated minorities of any sort. These are people made in the image of the God we serve and worship, and they should be treated with dignity, even if they choose lifestyles contrary to His ways. We fight on behalf of our neighbour, not for ourselves.

WISDOM AND PEACEMAKING

The final verse of James 3 really brings this whole theme home: *"And those who are peacemakers will plant seeds of peace and reap a harvest of righteousness"* (James 3:18, NLT). The wisdom from above produces fruit that ultimately contributes to peacemaking: meekness, purity, peace, gentleness, reasonableness/yielding, mercy, good fruits, impartiality, and sincerity (James 3:13, 17).

We must learn to respond in the wisdom from above when our rights and freedoms are violated instead of pursuing vengeance. When the rights and freedoms of those around us are violated, we seek justice for them, and we do it in the meekness of wisdom from above. Threats and revolution are not the way of the Kingdom.

This passage can almost seem to be disconnected from our overall train of thought. We were talking about wisdom, but now we're talking about a harvest? But Daniel made the same connection: *"And those who are wise shall shine like the brightness of the sky above; and those who turn many to righteousness, like the stars forever and ever"* (Daniel

12:3, emphasis added). Daniel equates those who are wise with those who turn many to righteousness.

When we stand and fight from our own anger, we act in earthly wisdom, which will never produce the righteousness of God we desire to see. Angrily ranting against government and the culture won't produce the revival so many pray for. Instead it's the peacemakers, the meek ones anchored in wisdom from above, who will see that harvest of righteousness.

When we respond in anger, we act in earthly, unspiritual, demonic wisdom. We're motivated by selfish ambition and jealousy, which often leads to compromises of integrity—half-truths or outright lies, stirring up trouble instead of making peace. None of these produce righteousness.

But when we are governed by the wisdom from above, we walk in meekness, living in confidence and filled with the Spirit of power, love, and self-control (2 Timothy 1:7). We can govern our bodies and speech, not subject to the fear of death (1 Corinthians 9:27, James 3:2, Revelation 12:11).

This is a picture of a truly powerful person (Proverbs 16:32, 25:28)—and as powerful people, we can choose to keep our swords in their sheaths when dealing with others. We don't fight for ourselves but look to stand for the rights of others and entrust our own vindication to God Himself.

James declares that it's the people who walk in the meekness of heavenly wisdom who will see answers to the prayers for a harvest of righteousness.

ESSENTIAL #8

Humility (James 4:1—5:12)

*God opposes the proud
but gives grace to the humble.*
(James 4:6)

In this chapter, we're going to cover a bigger chunk of James, and that's because one theme keeps coming up through it: humility. After imploring the believers to embrace and embody the meekness of wisdom, James gives his readers several examples of how to apply humility in their day-to-day lives. It appears this teaching was sorely needed, as James uses words like quarrels, fights, war, and murder to describe the relational dynamic in their communities (James 4:1–2).

This is a word for us today as well. We've all heard stories of, or experienced firsthand, quarrelling and fighting in the local church. Using words like war and murder might feel extreme, but James did say that the tongue *"is a restless evil, full of deadly poison"* (James 3:8).

As we saw in the last chapter, Solomon wrote that death and life are in the power of the tongue. And didn't Jesus include insults in His discussion on how to keep the command *"You shall not murder"* (Matthew 5:21)?

While we don't hear many reports of murder in the local church, thank God, I think we've all heard examples of people attacking or cutting down others with their words. The seed of murder can be found in such speech.

James was intentional in using these words to address the way early Christians related to one another. He clearly had zero tolerance for their quarrels and fights. Like Paul in Philippians 2 or Romans 12, James was eager to bring illumination and correction to the people's selfishness so they could finally look and act like one body.

The Holy Spirit is emphasizing the importance of unity once again in the body of Christ. Unity isn't primarily about us getting along so we can feel good, like achieving a sort of utopian harmony. Unity is a critical element to the success of the great commission. And the humility that fosters unity is essential for an effective prayer life.

THAT THEY MAY BE ONE

John 17 records exactly what Jesus prayed the night He was betrayed. In it, He mostly prays for His disciples, who were about to face the greatest test of their faith. But then He shifts His attention and prays *"for those who will believe in me through their word"* (John 17:20). That includes everyone who would come to saving faith in Jesus because of the gospel these apostles first carried. By extension, this includes all of us who believe today, according to the same faith that was once and for all delivered to the saints (Jude 3).

This means that we are among those He had in mind when He prayed this prayer.

In the prayer, Jesus asks the Father that we, the body of Christ, would become one:

> I do not ask for these [the eleven remaining disciples] only, but also for those who will believe in me through their word, that they may all be one, just as you, Father, are in me, and I in you, that they also may be in us, *so that the world may believe that you have sent me*. The glory that you have given me I have given to them, that they may be one even as we are one, I in them and you in me, that they may become perfectly one, *so that the world may know that you sent me and loved them even as you loved me*. (John 17:20–23, emphasis added)

Two factors in this prayer are quite incredible.

First, He prays for the church to experience a unity like the unity He enjoys with His Father: *"that they may all be one, just as you, Father, are in me, and I in you."* Think about that for a minute! How united are the Father and the Son?

We can look to the doctrine of the Trinity for this one. Though they are two distinct persons, together with the Holy Spirit they form one God. Their unity is such that, though they are three distinct persons, they are one entity.

The writer of Hebrews describes Jesus as *"the radiance of God's glory and the exact representation of his being"* (Hebrews 1:3, NIV). Earlier in the account of the last supper, Jesus told Philip, *"Whoever has seen me has seen the Father. How can you say, 'Show us the Father'? Do you not believe that I am in the Father and the Father is in me?"* (John 14:9–10) Jesus is so closely bound to the Father that to look at Him is to see the Father.

Jesus prayed that the unity among the church would somehow be like that.

The second incredible factor of this request is the effect it will have on our efforts in the great commission: *"That they may all be one, just as you, Father, are in me, and I in you, that they also may be in us, so that the world may believe that you have sent me."* That's right: Jesus says that the testimony of unity in the church is what will cause the world to believe that He is the one sent from the Father.

For good measure, Jesus repeats this idea twice in His prayer.

Earlier that evening, Jesus told His disciples about this dynamic when He gave them this clear charge:

> A new commandment I give to you, that you love one another: just as I have loved you, you also are to love one another. *By this all people will know that you are my disciples, if you have love for one another.* (John 13:34–35, emphasis added)

Again, this idea of loving unity in the church is about much more than us being comfortable with one another. It's an important component of our mission to make Him known!

As we discussed earlier, there are many divisions in the body today, many of which were created in the name of standing for truth. And yes, truth is non-negotiable. But we must be willing to wrestle through doctrinal differences with each other in a way that maintains the unity of the Spirit in the bond of peace (Ephesians 4:3).

Preaching alone won't open eyes and turn hearts. A diverse body of Christ that has genuine, godly, self-sacrificial love for one another will convince the world of the testimony of Jesus. With that in mind, we must find a way to wrestle and contend for truth with one another without resorting to burning bridges. After all, Revelation 19:7 and 22:17 make clear that Jesus is coming back for *one Bride*, not many churches or many believers.

Unity is a must for the church. Jesus won't return to a fractured Bride, but one that is pure, spotless, and unwrinkled, having made herself ready. This unity will be miraculous. It won't magically happen on its own; it will require our submission to the Holy Spirit and a willingness to seek the good of our neighbour before ourselves (1 Corinthians 10:24).

The single greatest characteristic that is required of us in this work is humility.

I think Paul would agree, as he made this argument in Philippians 2, pointing to Jesus as our pattern:

> …complete my joy by being of the same mind, having the same love, being in full accord and of one mind. Do nothing from selfish ambition or conceit, but in humility count others more significant than yourselves. Let each of you look not only to his own interests, but also to the interests of others… Have this mind among yourselves, which is yours in Christ Jesus, who, though he was in the form of God, did not count equality with God a thing to be grasped, but emptied himself, by taking the form of a servant, being born in the likeness of men. And being found in human form, he humbled

himself by becoming obedient to the point of death, even death on a cross. (Philippians 2:2–8)

Having the same posture of humility as Jesus is the key to a unified church.

It can feel like we're a long way away from John 17 being answered. Thankfully, it's not entirely up to us; the Holy Spirit is committed to bringing this about.

But this unity won't come easily. It is costly. Humility and pride are polar opposites, and the cost of unity is a humility that leaves no room for pride. In fact, it kills our pride. Isn't it worth it, though, to be able to offer Jesus the reward He died for? Isn't *He* worth it?

HUMILITY AND PRAYER

When we consider Jesus' desire for unity in His Bride, it should come as no surprise that the associated humility is also a key to effective prayer. In this context of addressing the schisms in the community of believers, James made his second statement on ineffective prayer: *"You ask and do not receive, because you ask wrongly, to spend it on your passions"* (James 4:3).

This connects to what we covered back in the first chapter. These believers' hearts were set on getting ahead in the world. We often think of money or material goods in this context, but what about influence, prestige, honour, or friends? We could add anything that would serve to make our lives more comfortable or successful. These things are good, but we turn them into idols when we pursue them first.

James' audience had prioritized their wants above loving God and neighbour. Not only had they fractured the body, but James says they had made themselves enemies of God by seeking to be friends with the world (James 4:4).

A couple of verses later, James cites the old proverb: *"God opposes the proud but gives grace to the humble"* (James 4:6). When we're caught up in ourselves, we find ourselves in opposition to God. How effective do you think such a prayer life would be?

This is not to say that God's affections for us change. His love for us remains constant. But He's not likely to greenlight many of our requests in that state.

In my own family, my sons have often wanted things that my wife and I know aren't beneficial for them, so we say no. Sometimes they take it as rejection or evidence that we don't love them, but the opposite is true! Our very love for them moves us to say no.

There are times when God allows us to catch the things we're chasing. But He often wrestles with us and our wayward desires, giving us leeway to chase after idols while also hedging our way in with thorns (Hosea 2:6).

Unanswered prayer can be an invitation to re-examine our motives. Sometimes it's an invitation to keep pressing in, but it sure doesn't hurt to revisit David's prayer for God to search him and know his heart (Psalm 139:23–24).

When we make ourselves enemies of God in our selfish pride, He opposes us. But He gives grace to the humble. We're more likely to pray the prayers that are on His heart when we maintain an attitude of humility.

We must get our desires in line with Him, seeking Him and His Kingdom before the things of this world: *"But seek first the kingdom of God and his righteousness, and all these things will be added to you"* (Matthew 6:33). That makes for effective prayer. When we're driven by selfish ambition and desires, damaging relationships in the process, it's a clue that we're not seeking His Kingdom and righteousness first.

Hopefully you can see something of the value of selflessness and unity within the body of Christ, and the humility required to achieve and maintain it.

Let's take some time to look at the various applications of humility James highlighted, considering how we can embrace them in our own lives. As we do, remember James' exhortation to the believers: *"But he gives more grace. Therefore it says, 'God opposes the proud but gives grace to the humble.' ...Humble yourselves before the Lord, and he will exalt you"* (James 4:6, 10). Humility keeps us in a posture that attracts the grace and power of God. This is especially true of our prayer lives.

ESSENTIAL #8: HUMILITY

HUMILITY IN REPENTANCE

As seems to be his way, James uses strong language to explain his readers' tendency to ask amiss (James 4:4–10). He doesn't merely suggest ways to pray but corrects a heart issue. When our hearts and passions are set on the wrong things, we actually oppose God. Just look at the words James uses to describe their status: adulterous, enmity, and enemy.

Please don't brush this point off or rush by it. Our goals and desires are of great significance to Him, though we can minimize their importance, especially if they are seemingly good goals.

We can easily see the problem if the pursuit is power, pleasure, and fame. But what about something noble and ministry-minded? For example, we can justify the pursuit of more social media likes, followers, and subscribers for our ministries in the name of advancing the gospel. But when that pursuit becomes our chief priority, where does that leave us? James appears to call that adultery and hostility toward God.

Jesus was clear that the things we treasure have the affections of our hearts (Matthew 6:19–24). If you want to know what you truly treasure, track how you invest your time, money, energy, and thoughts. When we prioritize other people or things, even good things, we work against God. This doesn't mean we forfeit our salvation or separate ourselves from the love of God, but it does mean that we're resisting Him instead of working with Him. We're playing tug-of-war with God instead of pulling in the same direction.

We need a revelation of the jealousy of God. He's not just happy you're here, glad that you're saved. James says, *"He yearns jealously over the spirit that he has made to dwell in us"* (James 4:5, emphasis added). He's not content with a part of us; He wants every part of us.

In the great theophany of Exodus 34, God declared to Moses that His very name is Jealous. You may be familiar with the declaration that God is a consuming fire, but do you know the rest of that verse? *"For the Lord your God is a consuming fire, a jealous God"* (Deuteronomy 4:24). A consuming fire describes the intensity of His jealousy. A jealous lover isn't content with a half-hearted response of love. He is only satisfied with a wholehearted response (Song of Solomon 8:6–7).

You might have a negative view of jealousy from stories of sinful men who went about this pursuit in all the wrong ways, violating the free will of those they pursued. But God's love is entirely pure, wholesome, and undefiled by sin. His pursuit of us is perfect. He fully honours our free will yet doesn't rest from pursuing us until He has our whole heart. He is merciful with us in our shortcomings and stumbling while pursuing us relentlessly. He won't let up until our selfishness and love for temporal comforts are out of the way, and He'll do it without once violating our free will.

This idea of the jealousy of God could strike you as overwhelming, and some of James' readers likely had the same thought. But James gave them good news: they weren't too far gone. Though they were steeped in selfish ambition, jealousy, and covetousness, he reminded them that God's supply of grace is greater than our weaknesses.

It's important to note that grace isn't just about God being nice. It's what empowers us to live differently. Paul makes clear in Romans 6–7 that the purpose of grace is not to give us permission to remain in sin; its purpose is to empower us to change, becoming more like Jesus, through the power of God working in us.

As we continue reading, James plainly describes how to access this grace: humility expressed through repentance.

Repentance is fundamentally an act of turning around. It begins with the acknowledgement of a wrong action or way of thinking, which requires humility. But more than acknowledging and saying sorry, repentance requires us to follow through by changing our thoughts and behaviour. Like faith, repentance is proven by actions (Matthew 3:8).

In James 4:7–8, James gives us three simple ways to walk out repentance.

The first is to submit to God. According to Merriam-Webster, this means "to yield oneself to the authority or will of another."[32] In other words, we don't argue or push back against His conviction but choose to submit to His leadership and agree with what He says.

---

[32] "Submit," *Merriam-Webster*. Date of access: July 9, 2024 (https://www.merriam-webster.com/dictionary/submit).

The second way is to resist the devil. This includes turning away from temptations, ruling over the sins that crouch at the door of our lives. We simply say no to temptation.[33]

The third way is to draw near to God. We do that by not fixating on the temptation we're trying to avoid, but turning our attention to the One who can satisfy our souls with superior pleasures (Psalm 16:11, 34:8, 36:8, 46:4, 103:5).

James calls his readers to humble themselves and acknowledge their issues—the selfish ambition, jealousy, and self-seeking that has produced fights and quarrels. To stubbornly deny the presence of those questionable heart motives is to remain in pride. This isn't the posture we want to take, because the terrifying reality is that God opposes the proud. He doesn't just disapprove of the proud; He *opposes* them, as they are at enmity with Him!

It is abundantly clear throughout Scripture that God loves the humble. They are the ones to whom He is drawn and responds (2 Samuel 22:28, Psalm 18:27, 147:6, 149:4, Proverbs 3:34, Isaiah 66:2, Matthew 18:4, 23:12, Luke 1:48, 52, James 4:6, 10, 1 Peter 5:6). We see this truth demonstrated in the lives of Old Testament kings who acted wickedly before the Lord but turned in repentance in the end; God showed even them mercy (1 Kings 21:29, 2 Kings 22:19, 2 Chronicles 7:14, 12:7, 12, 32:26, 33:12–13, 34:27).

The Bible is full of stories that show us how big a deal humility is to God. While He will always resist the proud, His preference is to show mercy and give grace. Humility and repentance open the door for that mercy and grace to come in.

We put ourselves at enmity with God when we pursue things of this age above Him and His Kingdom. We dig in further when, in pride, we ignore the conviction of the Holy Spirit. God opposes those who stand in their pride, but He comes with grace to the ones who humble themselves—grace to turn around, to get our desires in line with His, to seek first His Kingdom and His righteousness, and to entrust all the other

---

[33] The phrase "resist the devil" is sometimes used to support a practice of rebuking and binding all sorts of powers and principalities in prayer. That's not really what this passage is getting at, though. It's about resisting temptation, turning from our sinful desires.

stuff to Him. He will empower us to make the changes, but we must humble ourselves and take the first step in repentance.

James encourages his readers to embrace repentance: *"Be wretched and mourn and weep. Let your laughter be turned to mourning and your joy to gloom"* (James 4:9). Not an exciting verse, I know. But here's the beauty of the gospel: it's an exchange, with a very generous exchange rate. Isaiah 61 tells us that our mourning is exchanged for comfort and the oil of gladness, our ashes for a crown of beauty, and our shame for a double portion of honour.

Jesus has dealt with all our filthy sin, and He is well-pleased to clothe us with garments of salvation and robes of righteousness, best described as an exquisite, lavish wedding dress (Isaiah 61:10). Repentance is the act by which we bring Him our mourning, ashes, and shame so we can receive His comfort, honour, and beautiful garments. This means that repentance isn't negative; it's the doorway to all the benefits of the new covenant!

In Luke 7:36–50, Jesus tells a parable of two debtors. One owed the creditor five hundred denarii and the other owed him fifty. A denarius was generally one day's wages, so for us today this could be like a minimum wage earner owing $60,000, and the other owing $6,000. In the parable, the creditor forgave the debts of both.

Jesus asks which debtor would have a greater response of love. The obvious answer is the one who was forgiven the larger debt.

We know that all have sinned and fall short of the glory of God, that none of us are capable of producing true righteousness, and that if we sin in one area of the law we are a transgressor of the entire law (Romans 3:23, Isaiah 64:6, James 2:10).

As it relates to this parable, both debtors were equally guilty. The difference is that the one who owed more would have been more acutely aware of his desperate situation. He likely experienced more fear, anxiety, and stress. Thus, when the pardon came, his relief would have been greater.

By inviting his readers to *"be wretched, mourn and weep,"* James encourages us not to make light of our sin, but to let the weight of it touch our hearts. Does he say this so we would walk around feeling terrible about ourselves? No! He wants us to be aware of the extent and effect of our sins so the exchange of repentance might produce a greater response of love and gratitude. The one who has been forgiven of much will love much; the one who is forgiven little loves little (Luke 7:47).

This is the invitation: when confronted with your sin, don't hide from it. God isn't laying a guilt trip on you (Romans 8:1–2, 2 Corinthians 7:10). He's providing an invitation for you to experience His mercy and walk in a greater measure of His grace.

David acknowledged that sorrow does last for a night, but there's a promise of joy in the morning; though we may feel His anger for a moment, His favour lasts a lifetime (Psalm 30:5). Embrace humility, acknowledge sin when the Holy Spirit convicts you of it, and receive all that He longs to give you in the glorious exchange that happens when we come to Him in repentance. It is the doorway to grace.

ADDRESSING ARROGANCE

In the latter half of the fourth chapter, James addresses arrogant attitudes that can creep in if we're not watchful. The first arrogance deals with how we view and think about our brothers and sisters. Our tendency is to look at things our fellow believers do and conclude whether we agree or disagree with them, whether we think they're right or wrong. James raises a big red flag for us here:

> The one who speaks against a brother or judges his brother, speaks evil against the law and judges the law. *But if you judge the law, you are not a doer of the law but a judge.* There is only one lawgiver and judge, he who is able to save and to destroy. *But who are you to judge your neighbor?* (James 4:11–12, emphasis added)

His point is this: when we start passing judgment on a brother or sister, we start to see ourselves as the judge who oversees the administration of the law, not as one subject to it ourselves. Of course we need to be discerning, testing every doctrine and confronting sin, but that doesn't give us permission to do so with a critical, judgmental spirit that assumes the worst of others.

We contend for truth while making every effort to maintain the unity of the Spirit in the bond of peace by bearing with one another in love. When we see a difference or perceive something to be off-course, we must attempt to come to the knowledge of the truth together before writing one another off.

This is a repetition of James' encouragement to *"receive with meekness the implanted word, which is able to save your souls"* (James 1:21). We need to remember that our first job is not to apply the Word to everyone else, but to apply it to ourselves, to not see ourselves as above the law or think of ourselves more highly than we should. The point is, always address the plank in your own eye before trying to remove a speck from your brother's (Matthew 7:1–5).

When there's an issue with blatantly wrong doctrine or harmful practices, yes, those need to be dealt with. In my experience, correction is always best received in the context of genuine friendship. Think about it. If someone's going to call you out for a pattern of sinful behaviour, who's more likely to get your attention: a complete stranger or a friend or mentor who has walked with you through thick and thin?

As we saw earlier, Matthew 18 makes it clear that the purpose of confrontation is to win back the heart of your brother, not to win an argument. How can you win back a heart you never had to begin with?

We should also consider what Paul says in Romans 14:1–12. He makes the point that we're all servants of God, and servants are judged by their Master. We aren't judged by other servants. So yes, contend for truth, but also bear with one another in love. Wrestle through disagreements.

If you don't come to an agreement, be wary of crossing that line of pronouncing judgment. That's not our place. As James 4:12 tells us, *"There is only one lawgiver and judge, he who is able to save and to destroy."* Instead we must keep a healthy measure of humility through difficult conversations.

Even the great apostle Paul had humility in this matter. When he spoke of being compared to Apollos and evaluated by the Corinthians, he said, *"My conscience is clear, but that doesn't prove I'm right"* (1 Corinthians 4:4, NLT, emphasis added). We all hold to our convictions because we believe them to be true. But if Paul could acknowledge the possibility of having gotten some things wrong, maybe we could have some of that humility, too.

All I'm trying to do here is bring some balance to the discussion of how to deal with a brother we perceive to be in error. In this era of cancel culture, it's easy to throw stones and write off people we disagree with. My appeal is that we wouldn't rush to that step with a judgmental spirit but do what we can to hold as tightly to the unity of the body as we do to truth. Jesus believed a unified church was worth dying for, so it must be important.

The second arrogance James addresses sounds a lot like what John called the *"pride of life"* (1 John 2:16). James reminds us that our lives are little more than vapour in the grand scheme of things before the eternal God. It's easy to make our plans and assume we'll get to do everything we want, but James encourages us to be mindful of the fact that we draw every breath from God. Instead of presuming that we can do whatever we plan, even if those plans are good and Kingdom-related, he suggests we add the caveat *"If the Lord wills"* (James 4:15).

James can sound overbearing on this point, but again, the heart of it is humility. Acknowledging that we're dependent on another for life and breath is foundational for a humble heart. When we recognize that life itself is a gift, then everything we do with that life is planned with humility and gratitude. When we ignore this fact and think we can do whatever we want, whenever we want, James suggests we're boasting, arrogant, and evil. Keep a humble, grateful, worshipful posture before the Creator and Sustainer of your life.

ADDRESSING INJUSTICE

In James 5, James applies this idea of humility to the topic of injustice, both to those suffering under injustice and those perpetrating injustice. It's terrible to think there would be a need to call out Christians for this behaviour, but unfortunately that's the case far too often.

His case is against the rich ones among the believers, specifically those who amass their fortunes on the backs of exploited labourers. Once again, he uses jarring, no-holds-barred language in imploring them to repent of this practice.

We can draw a few points from this passage.

First, the issue once again is of misplacing our treasures. Instead of living mindful of His Kingdom and righteousness, these people's eyes are solely fixed on the wealth they can amass in this lifetime; it's like they have dollar signs in their eyes. While money itself isn't awful, we know that the love of money is the root of all kinds of evil (1 Timothy 6:10). These people's desire for money leads them to disregard the cries of the very ones they benefit from.

James uses strong language to help them recognize the seriousness of the issue and their need to repent: *"Come now, you rich, weep and howl for the miseries that are coming upon you"* (James 5:1).

Second, he addresses the mistaken belief that God couldn't see this behaviour or didn't care. If we erroneously believe that God is standing at the ready to strike a sinner with lightning, we can be fooled into believing that anything that isn't stopped must be okay.

Similarly, the believers James wrote to may have misinterpreted God's longsuffering for a blessing on their endeavours.

Author and speaker Bob Sorge once noted,

> One of the clear messages from the book of Job: Never assume that blessing means God's favor, or that calamity means God's disapproval. The cross is the greatest example of that truth. The lonely, tortured figure on the tree was actually the most favored one on the hill.[34]

Just because those rich believers seemed to get away with their injustices doesn't mean they were right with God. As we have already seen,

---

[34] Bob Sorge, *Facebook*. August 25, 2019 (https://www.facebook.com/BobSorgeMinistry/posts/pfbid02PVFDbf1MdeEcnAgAqeaxUHqcR5cVbyAY4KUKTH2zpEQCi4F-NEi8cuikiPhpeJkJHl).

God sees and hears the plight of the poor and oppressed, and He acts on their behalf. We've also seen that we will all stand to give an account as servants before our Master, who happens to be the one Lawgiver and Judge.

Never mistake God's longsuffering for indifference.

Third, James' choice of language indicates the weight injustices carry before God: *"Behold, the wages of the laborers who mowed your fields, which you kept back by fraud, are crying out against you, and the cries of the harvesters have reached the ears of the Lord of hosts"* (James 5:4).

Does some of that wording sound familiar? It's eerily similar to the language used to describe Abel's blood crying out from the ground after Cain killed him (Genesis 4:1–16). We would obviously judge murder to be more egregious than some withheld wages, but James seems to argue that God is just as displeased with a heart that seeks to exploit a fellow man. James even declares that these rich men have effectively condemned and murdered those more righteous than them (James 5:6).

When it comes to leadership, Scripture has given us a crystal-clear template to follow. It primarily involves serving those under our care, not exploiting them for personal gain (Ezekiel 34, Matthew 20:25, John 10, 13:1–15, Mark 10:45). If you're in a position of leadership, whether that be in the local church, a parachurch ministry, the workplace, or at home, invite the Holy Spirit to reveal any areas where you can grow in humility and root out injustice. Let's seek to be shepherds after His own heart (Jeremiah 3:15).

Finally, James addresses the believers who were suffering under injustice. This one isn't so comfortable for us in the West. The words that jump off the page are patience, suffering, and perseverance (or endurance); they are most applicable in seasons of trials and tribulations. You know, seasons we're not used to.

James gives three commands here: to be patient (James 5:7), establish your hearts and remain patient (James 5:8), and not grumble (James 5:9). With all three of these commands, he points to one common hope as a reason to endure: the coming of the Lord, for *"the Judge is standing at the door"* (James 5:9). In other words, "Hang in there! He is coming soon, and He will make it right!"

Once again, this idea is tied to where our treasure is. If we live with an eye toward being successful in this life, we will have a difficult time patiently enduring suffering because it doesn't line up with success. What preserved those early believers through persecution was the knowledge that the Lord will return and bring His reward with Him (Isaiah 62:11, Revelation 22:12).

This isn't to say that things can't change, or that He won't miraculously intervene in the here and now; there are many stories throughout church history of divine deliverance from real danger. But the knowledge that He is alive and returning gave people the resolve to persevere even if He didn't come through in the present, just like the three Hebrews thrown in the fiery furnace (Daniel 3:16–18). The long and short of their story is that they valued Him and His rewards more than this life.

James gives two examples for us, the first being the prophets. Everyone loves the prophets. They prophesied with remarkable accuracy about the purposes of God in their generations and the generations to come. They delivered powerful messages about the fiery, passionate love of God for His people.

But most of the prophets were hated in their time. Jeremiah faced strong opposition and got thrown in a well, left for dead. Ezekiel faced so much opposition that the Lord had to harden his will so he wouldn't back down. Daniel served his entire life in the courts of demon-worshiping kings. Hebrew legend has it, perhaps supported by Hebrews 11:37, that Isaiah was martyred, sawn in two.

We love their words in hindsight, but in the days of their ministries these prophets were vehemently opposed. Nobody likes hearing that they need to change.

But why do we love them and their messages today? James says that it's because they endured to the end, refusing to recant or retract: *"Behold, we consider those blessed who remained steadfast"* (James 5:11). He implies that the prophets' heroism was tied to their ability to endure and remain steadfast.

The other example is Job, who suffered an incredible barrage of sorrow and pain. He lost his many children, massive wealth, and health all in a very short span of time. To make matters worse, his wife wasn't exactly encouraging; her advice was to curse God and die (Job 2:9).

But the Word tells us that he didn't accuse God of wrongdoing. He wisely kept his mouth shut (Job 1:22, 2:10).

Through most of his book, Job wrestles with the question any of us would ask in those circumstances: "Why, God?" He couldn't see what God saw through it all, but he held on as long as he could. Notice James' hindsight assessment of Job's situation: *"you have seen the purpose of the Lord, how the Lord is compassionate and merciful"* (James 5:11).

Suffering is never the end of the story for us. Suffering was never going to be the end of the story for Job, but he didn't know that in the middle of his suffering. When we face trials, we usually don't see the light at the end of the tunnel. Many in church history have referred to these seasons as dark nights of the soul. In such times, do we throw our hands up, curse God, and walk away in self-preservation? Or do we endure patiently?

James tells us that it was God's purpose to shower Job with compassion and mercy again; indeed, Job wound up richer in the end than he had been before his testing.

A good friend of mine, Daryl Betts, loves this saying: "God is doing more behind our back than He is in front of our face." We don't often see it in the process, but He is constantly working all things together for good. Even suffering works for our good, escorting us to a place of deeper intimacy with Him, and it works to prepare an eternal weight of glory for us later (Philippians 3:10, 2 Corinthians 4:17, Romans 8:17–18). It's amazing how many times I've heard people say, "It was the hardest thing I've ever had to go through. But because of what God did in me through that season, I'd do it all over again."

We may not see it today, but when He returns and we see in full, I think we'll look back and see suffering as a gift.

THE DIFFERENCE BETWEEN THEN AND NOW

There's one other point we should take from this passage. James wrote his letter to people who didn't have the rights, freedoms, and privileges we enjoy today. Even with the shifting sands of culture, we still have freedoms of conscience, belief, religion, and speech protected by law.

They did not. As worshipers of another Lord and Saviour, those Christians were outcasts in their society, and many suffered torture and death for refusing to burn incense before a statue of the emperor.[35] They were essentially outlaws; their worship of Jesus was illegal. James' encouragements showed them how to keep their hearts from offence and remain faithful to the end.

For us today, we have legal recourse. We hear an increasing number of stories in our country of people being charged or removed from places of work or education for holding to a biblical worldview. Yet in all these situations, we still have legal recourse. It's not easy or comfortable, and it's very expensive, but it's still there. There are tools we can use.

Our situation is actually similar to the apostle Paul's. Paul had the benefit of being born a Roman citizen, and he was never shy about playing that card (Acts 22:24–28). He held the magistrates of Philippi accountable when they beat him and Silas without trial. He got out of a flogging by citing his Roman citizenship, and he appealed his case all the way up the judicial chain to Caesar (Acts 16:35–40, 22:24–29, 25:11).

The remarkable thing is that as Paul held court with the various governors and kings on his way up that ladder, he never lashed out in anger over his unjust imprisonment or demanded his freedom. Instead he took the opportunity to preach the gospel to each and every one, contending for their salvation!

We see this plainly at the end of Acts 26, where King Agrippa could plainly perceive that Paul sought to convert him. He said in private that Paul would have been set free if he hadn't appealed to Caesar. Paul wasn't concerned for his freedom, rights, or privileges, but hoped *"to God that not only you but also all who hear me this day might become such as I am— except for these chains"* (Acts 26:29).

With Paul's example in mind, James' instructions are still very applicable to how we carry our hearts through similar challenges. We are to walk through the troubles we face with patience (James 5:7). We are

---

[35] Donna R. Ridge and E. Ray Clendenen, "Emperor Worship," *Holman Illustrated Bible Dictionary* (Nashville, TN: Holman Bible Publishers, 2003).

to establish our hearts through trouble, so that we aren't easily shaken (James 5:8). We are to hold our tongues, refraining from grumbling (James 5:9). We pursue justice with the tools at our disposal, but on the heart level we entrust the idea of vengeance to the Lord's hands, refusing to repay evil with evil (Romans 12:17–21).

This concept can be a bit foreign to us, but it's important that we learn and practice it now. It doesn't take a prophet to read the cultural winds and see trouble on the horizon for people who are loyal to Jesus and His Word (if things don't change). We each need to settle the question in our own hearts of what we treasure most. If we esteem comfort, influence, popularity, money, and even family more than we esteem Him, His promises, and His rewards, it will be difficult for us to remain faithful to Jesus.

Jesus warned that many would be led astray, many would fall away, and the love of many would grow cold before His return (Matthew 24:4, 10, 12). We would be wise to settle this question in our hearts now, before the pressure increases.

ALL ABOUT HUMILITY

In all these things—repentance, refraining from judging our brothers, being grateful for life, treating those under us well, and enduring hardship with patience—humility is at the core.

One of Jesus' most well-loved statements reads, *"Come to me, all who labour and are heavy laden, and I will give you rest"* (Matthew 11:28). This assures us of finding rest from an unbearable burden by laying it at His feet.

But He didn't leave it at that. He didn't say, "Drop your load and be done with it." He told us that there's a better, more sustainable way to live: *"Take my yoke upon you, and <u>learn from me, for I am gentle and lowly in heart</u>, and you will find rest for your souls"* (Matthew 11:29, emphasis added).

Note that the Greek words translated as gentle and lowly can also be translated as meek and humble. Jesus, in calling us to Himself, is inviting us to learn how to be meek and humble, like Him. The One who will inherit all the kingdoms of the earth and shepherd them with a rod of iron was prophesied to be the One who wouldn't raise His voice to get attention, break a bruised reed, or snuff out a flickering candle (Isaiah 42:1–4).

Jesus' life was an example of meekness, of power under restraint. Paul's ministry to Corinth was the same; he didn't come to sway them with powerful orations and impressive wisdom. In fact, he appeared weak and even fearful, but demonstrations of the Spirit and power were present (1 Corinthians 2:3–5).

These are the types of lives that turned the first-century world upside-down. They were meek and humble toward men, but their prayers shook the earth, advancing the gospel of the Kingdom in the power of the Spirit.

And there it is: humility is an essential for effective prayer, humility before God and humility lived out with one another in the body of Christ. He opposes the proud but gives grace to the humble.

ESSENTIAL #9

Fervent and Righteous (James 5:13–20)

*The prayer of a righteous person has
great power as it is working.*
(James 5:16)

As we reach the conclusion of James' letter, he closes with some final encouragements regarding prayer. Given his reputation, that shouldn't come as a surprise.

Let's recall that in both previous passages where James talked about prayer, he commented on what makes our prayers ineffective. Now we're going to hear what he has to say about effective prayer. We'll briefly acknowledge some of James' first encouragements about prayer before really drilling down into the substance of it.

He starts by encouraging the believers to pray and interact with God, whatever season they're in. He writes, paraphrased, "Are you suffering? Pray! Is life good right now? Praise Him! Are you sick? Pray, and get others, especially the elders, to pray for you, too!"

Quite simply: pray, pray, pray! This echoes Paul's exhortations to lift our voices to Him in everything, whether we're asking in need, giving thanks for what He's done, or rejoicing in who He is (Philippians 4:6–7, 1 Thessalonians 5:16–18).

The next line brings us to the precipice of the final point we will consider: *"Confess your sins to each other and pray for each other so that you may be healed"* (James 5:16, NLT). James connects the act of confessing our sins to one another with effective prayer. This pattern blends well with John's words from 1 John 1:5–10, where acknowledgement and confession of sin contribute to healthy fellowship with other believers, walking in the light as He is in the light, and being cleansed.

But if we pretend there is nothing to confess, we remain stuck where we are.

This idea of being cleansed from all unrighteousness (1 John 1:9), associated with the confession of our sins, leads us to James' most well-known statement on prayer: *"The prayer of a righteous person has great power as it is working"* (James 5:16). Here we have James' thesis statement on effective prayer.

Let's first consider that this verse is translated a number of different ways. There are many variations: *"the effective, fervent prayer of a righteous man"* (NKJV), *"the effective prayer of a righteous man"* (NASB), *"the earnest prayer of a righteous person"* (NLT), *"the heartfelt and persistent prayer of a righteous man"* (AMP), etc.

It seems like the words fervent or effective often get the bulk of the attention in this verse. But don't lose sight of the one word that appears in each translation: *righteous*. I think that's the key word.

The prayer of the righteous is emphasized, not the degree of zeal or fervour behind the prayer. In fact, the New International Version and English Standard Version skip fervent and effective altogether, noting only that it is the prayer of a righteous person that is powerful. This is because James used the Greek word *deesis*, which is translated as prayer, but it also includes the ideas of a plea, request, or petition.[36]

James didn't use a Greek word for fervent or earnest. He didn't specify fervency here, but some translators have added it to highlight the pleading sense of *deesis*. This is to say that I think James is emphasizing the words prayer and righteous.

When we read on, we see that the words fervently, or earnestly, show up in the next verse, describing Elijah's prayers that both instigated and concluded a drought in Israel's history. If we take a closer look at the wording, we might be surprised by James' idea of fervency.

FERVENCY AND PRAYER

To define fervour, most English dictionaries use words like passion, intensity, zeal, or enthusiasm. When we read James 5:16 from that

---

[36] James Swanson, *A Dictionary of Biblical Languages: Greek New Testament*, #1255.

ESSENTIAL #9: FERVENT *and* RIGHTEOUS

understanding, we may imagine someone praying loudly, energetically, and enthusiastically. That isn't necessarily wrong, but it doesn't reflect the primary understanding of fervency James is communicating here.

The next verse reads, *"Elijah was a man with a nature like ours, and he prayed fervently that it might not rain…"* (James 5:17) When we look at the Greek again, we don't find a word for fervently, usually *ekteneia*, or *zeo*, in the New Testament. The words that get translated to "prayed fervently" are *proseuxato* and *proseuche*.

You probably notice that these are similar words.

Proseuxato is a form of *proseuchomai*, and its definition is "pray."[37] This word is used eighty-five times in the New Testament and is always translated to some form of pray (prayed, prayer, praying, prayers, etc.).

The definition of *proseuche* is "prayer" or "place for prayer," and it appears thirty-six times in the New Testament.[38] But there's a catch here: every time it's used, it's translated as prayer or prayers—that is, every time except for James 5. This is the only time it's translated as fervently.

What does this mean? If we look at it in a word-for-word sense, James is saying that Elijah "prayed prayers" that it wouldn't rain. Alternatively, we could use a phrase like "Elijah prayed and prayed."

Here's the point: James isn't emphasizing that Elijah prayed excitedly, loudly, or with lots of volume. He is emphasizing that Elijah prayed with endurance and persistence, not giving up. Again, in these two verses the Greek words generally translated to fervently, or earnestly, simply do not appear.

Paul did say that we shouldn't be lazy in our walk with the Lord, but *"fervent in spirit"* (Romans 12:11), and Luke complimentarily described Apollos as being *"fervent in spirit"* (Acts 18:25). I'm not knocking that idea at all. But when it comes to prayer, Scripture generally emphasizes endurance over enthusiasm. And doesn't it make sense that James would emphasize that persistence, given that he earned the nickname Old Camel Knees because of the long hours he spent in prayer?

We in the Western church tend to think that the more expressive and enthusiastic someone is, the more spiritual, radical, or "on fire" they

---

[37] Ibid., #4667.
[38] Ibid., #4666.

are. Sometimes there's a correlation between the two. We naturally get excited and passionate in seasons when we're drawing nearer to God or seeing Him move. That often happens over a couple of weeks, maybe months.

But for most people, big and loud expressions of zeal aren't part of their makeup. It's not a part of normal, everyday life. If they were to act like that all the time, their conscience would question whether they were being authentic. Still, we sometimes think that the louder and more excitable ones are the most fervent.

I don't know about you, but I've had seasons when I've wondered whether my love for God was genuine because I wasn't as outwardly pumped as those around me. I felt pressure to ramp up my enthusiasm, and if I refused I felt a bit of shame for not being zealous enough.

If we ramp up the enthusiasm on our own, without it naturally arising from a work of the Spirit in our hearts, all we're manufacturing is hype and striving.

I recently wrestled with this conundrum. I was comparing myself to other believers who I considered to be more dedicated, more fervent, more radical than me. Our church had been conducting a study on the letters to the churches in Revelation at the time, and I found myself reading the letter to the Philadelphians. Of the seven letters, this is one of only two where Jesus didn't offer a correction or rebuke.

I nearly moved on from the letter because I didn't believe I could relate to it. I thought I should be reading the letter to Ephesus, being called back to my first love. Or the letter to Thyatira, being warned about compromise. Or the letter to Sardis, since I don't always feel as vibrant in my faith as some people seem to think I do.

But I couldn't shake the sense that the Holy Spirit wanted me to read the Philadelphia letter again. When I did, the eighth verse jumped off the page at me:

> I know your works. Behold, I have set before you an open door, which no one is able to shut. *I know that you have but little power, and yet you have kept my*

ESSENTIAL #9: FERVENT and RIGHTEOUS

word and have not denied my name. (Revelation 3:8, emphasis added)

Jesus commended the Philadelphians not because they were big, strong, or impressive, but because they hadn't quit. They had a little strength, not a lot. In the face of persecution, they had remained faithful to His Word and to His name. He encouraged and commended them for their patient endurance (Revelation 3:10). In other words, their fervency looked like endurance, and Jesus commended them for it.

When Paul knew he was nearing the end of his life, he wrote, *"I have fought the good fight, I have finished the race, I have kept the faith"* (2 Timothy 4:7). He had encouraged the Corinthians to run their own race with the intention of winning (1 Corinthians 9:24), and that was five to ten years earlier. Still thinking along the lines of running a race, Paul declared that he was about to finish his. He didn't define his run as successful because he stayed zealous or accomplished many things, but by the fact that he had kept the faith. He had endured to the end, remaining faithful.

We often think that radical Christianity has to look like fervency and zeal all the time, but that's not the proper measuring stick. What heaven celebrates is the one who remains faithful, growing from glory to glory until we finally appear before Him (Psalm 84:5–7, Romans 4:19–22, 2 Corinthians 3:18, Hebrews 11). Fervent Christianity looks like staying steady through both the highs and lows. That's the type of fervency James endorses.

We see this same emphasis on persistence, faithfulness, or endurance in other passages that talk about prayer. Jesus specified that God will answer His elect who cry out to Him day and night with speedy justice (Luke 18:7–8).

Crying out day and night in prayer requires endurance. When Jesus asked Peter, James, and John to watch with Him in prayer in Gethsemane, He didn't ask for excitement but endurance. He wanted them to resist their urge to sleep and watch with Him (Matthew 26:36–41).

Paul encouraged the Thessalonians to *"pray without ceasing"* (1 Thessalonians 5:17).

Perhaps one of the most striking examples is seen in Isaiah 62:

> On your walls, O Jerusalem, I have set watchmen; *all the day and all the night they shall never be silent.* You who put the Lord in remembrance, *take no rest, and give him no rest until* he establishes Jerusalem and makes it a praise in the earth. (Isaiah 62:6–7, emphasis added)

This is clearly a promise that God will raise up watchmen who won't stop reminding Him of His promises until He has established Jerusalem as a *"praise in the earth"*—all day and all night. That's endurance.

While God certainly isn't against enthusiasm, it appears that He is primarily interested in a fervency marked by lasting consistency.

Returning to James 5, we see this point made in the very example James uses. He references Elijah, who *"prayed fervently that it might not rain, and for three years and six months it did not rain on the earth. Then he prayed again, and heaven gave rain, and the earth bore its fruit"* (James 5:17–18).

Let's consider that story. Elijah appears on the scene in 1 Kings 17. The first we see of him is in King Ahab's court, declaring an indefinite drought which would end only at his word. We aren't told anything about the prayer work that was done leading up to that proclamation, or during the three and a half years of drought. Based on the examples noted above, I would assume that he kept praying concerning that drought while it continued, but that would admittedly be speculation. So we basically go by James' word here, concluding that Elijah's fervent prayer was a catalyst in bringing about the drought.

Later in 1 Kings 17, during the drought, Elijah is sent to live as a guest with a widow in Zarephath, well outside Israel's borders. During his time there, the widow's son died. Elijah prayed for the boy three times, until he came back to life. Three times! How many of us would have the faith and audacity to continue praying for resurrection after having prayed with desperation twice to no avail? That's perseverance!

Then we see the differing ideas of fervency demonstrated in the climactic event that brought an end to the drought. In 1 Kings 18, Elijah called for all of Israel to assemble at Mount Carmel, where he and the prophets of Baal would have a showdown: they would each call on their god to answer with fire, and the one who did would be recognized as the one true God.

Elijah allowed the four hundred fifty prophets of Baal (and four hundred of Asherah) to go first. They built an altar, prepared a sacrifice, and danced and prayed all morning until they were hobbled with fatigue. Elijah started mocking them around noon, and that's when their fervency really kicked in: they got louder, started mutilating themselves, and *"raved all afternoon until the time of the evening sacrifice"* (1 Kings 18:29, NLT). They prayed with exceptional fervency, both enthusiastic and enduring, but to no avail.

Then came Elijah's turn. When I read this passage, one word stands out in describing Elijah's actions in comparison with the actions of the prophets of Baal. It's a very plain, simple word: *said*.

The word said sounds more like talking, especially when compared with the shouting and raving of the prophets of Baal. When we read 1 Kings 18:30, we see that Elijah spoke (said) to the people of Israel four times: once for them to gather around, and then three separate times to pour water on the sacrificial bull.

Said is an insignificant word, but it sure seems to imply that Elijah was more calm than wound up. 1 Kings 18:30 also says that he, by himself, repaired and rebuilt the altar of the Lord that lay in ruins there. Picture one guy piling rocks while thousands and thousands watched. It's not very exciting. Maybe he worked at it while the prophets of Baal were carrying on. In any case, it may have been suspenseful, but it sure doesn't sound like it was exuberant.

When it came time for his prayer, it was more of the same: *"And at the time of the offering of the oblation, Elijah the prophet came near and <u>said</u>, 'O Lord, God of Abraham, Isaac, and Israel...'"* (1 Kings 18:36, emphasis added) This verse doesn't say that he cried out, lifted his voice, or shouted. It's reasonable to assume that he used a loud enough voice for the people around him to hear, but the scripture doesn't explicitly tell us. We only read that he *said* his prayer. God heard that prayer and answered with fire.

In the final portion of the story, Elijah prayed for rain to come and the drought to end. He climbed to the top of the mountain, bowed down with his face between his knees, and began praying. After a time, he asked his servant whether he had seen anything yet. The answer was no, but Elijah kept praying.

Six times the answer was no.[39] It wasn't until the seventh time that Elijah finally got the answer he was looking for: *"I saw a little cloud about the size of a man's hand rising from the sea"* (1 Kings 18:44, NLT). Elijah kept on praying—he prayed and prayed—until his servant could see a cloud forming on the horizon. The rains came, and the drought was over.

When we read this story, we get a clearer picture of persistent prayer than we do of exuberant prayer. It was Elijah's persistent fervour that secured the breakthrough.

The same is true for us today. God is looking for those who will watch with Him, who will give Him no rest, who will cry out to Him night and day. In other words, those who will pray without ceasing.

Just like Jacob, who wrestled with the angel through the night and refused to let go until he received a blessing (Genesis 32:22–32), God loves it when we persevere in prayer and don't let go of Him. This isn't because we have to convince God to do something; rather, it's for our benefit. It has been said that prayer is not an exercise in overcoming God's reluctance, but in realizing His willingness. We come to know Him and His heart much better the longer we tarry or wrestle with Him. That's the fervency that really delights Him.

This doesn't mean that praying loudly or enthusiastically is wrong. It's good to press in with all our heart. That is part of loving Him with all our strength and mind. If you're naturally expressive and outgoing, don't change anything! This encouragement is especially meant for those who are quieter by nature, and maybe feel less spiritual because of it. You don't have to get loud and rowdy for God to hear you or be moved by your prayer. Effective prayer isn't measured by volume. Don't be shy.

---

[39] I have trouble believing that Elijah would have been offering short "Please send rain" prayers and then checking. His bowed posture seems to indicate that he was pressing in with his prayer, not passive or disengaged.

ESSENTIAL #9: FERVENT *and* RIGHTEOUS

Don't draw back. He loves the sound of your voice. But you don't have to be loud for God to hear you or for your prayer to be effective.

The main takeaway is that the most important kind of fervent prayer is the one that's enduring, persistent, and continuous, regardless of expression.

I'll also add that it's not about how effective we can make our prayers through strategies or specific verbiage. When we reduce prayer to a formula—"I say this, now You do that"—we can slip into a mindset of works—or at worse, control and manipulation. We cannot earn answers to prayer for saying the right things, nor can we force God into a corner and make Him do what we want Him to do. Prayer isn't about finding the right combination of words to finally force God's hand to move in our favour, but about tarrying with Him.

Again, we aren't overcoming a reluctance on His part, but staying in the process with Him until we realize His willingness.

SIDE NOTE: PRAYING FOR JUDGMENT

In this passage, James specifically references the three-and-a-half-year drought in Israel that began and ended because of Elijah's earnest prayers. The heavens once again rained down, allowing the earth to bear its fruit, once Elijah reversed course and prayed for rain. Elijah was a normal person, just like us, and he saw God miraculously answer his bold prayers.

We read this example and see that Elijah prayed for judgment, by way of withholding rain, and God answered this prayer. We know from this and other passages that there are times when the people of God partner with Him in releasing His judgments on the earth (Psalm 149:5–9, Matthew 10:14–15, Revelation 6:9–10). The Bible is clear that at times God moves in judgment, and the saints have a role in partnering with Him in prayer toward that end. But we must keep these passages in balance with others.

God's desire is that not one soul should perish, but that all would come to repentance. He delights in showing mercy, and wherever possible mercy triumphs over judgment (2 Peter 3:9, 1 Timothy 2:1–4,

Micah 7:18, James 2:13). He is slow to anger, abounding in love. He by no means clears the guilty.

But notice this: sins can be dealt with for three to four generations, where there is continued rebellion against Him (Deuteronomy 5:9). And yet His steadfast love is poured out to a thousand generations (Exodus 34:6–7). The Bible makes clear that His priority is to show mercy instead of judgment, wherever possible. The ultimate demonstration of this is seen in Jesus' voluntary, substitutionary death on the cross: He preferred to bear man's punishment than leave man to bear it himself.[40]

Too often believers wish for failure and calamity to come upon people who oppose them, or even just plain disagree with them, especially when it comes to political parties and leaders. We've already unpacked how Jesus called us to respond differently. The point is that God delights in showing mercy (Micah 7:18), so we ought to prefer it and pray for it, too.

Consider the example of the northern kingdom of Israel in the Old Testament. From the day they split from the southern kingdom of Judah, the northern kingdom never sought the Lord again. In 1 Kings 12, King Jeroboam established a religion for this breakaway kingdom featuring two golden calves, temples on high places, and a new priesthood. The motivation was largely political. Jeroboam didn't want the people of Israel travelling to Judah's capital, Jerusalem, for annual feasts. He didn't want them defecting to Judah. As a result, the ten tribes of northern Israel descended into idol worship and never again truly sought the Lord as a nation.

How long do you think God put up with their apostasy? After all, this was the nation He had set apart as a special possession to Himself out of all the nations, demonstrating His glory and power on their behalf and establishing covenants with them. To whom much is given, much is required (Luke 12:48); the bar of righteousness and obedience was high for these people.

---

[40] Note that the Word is clear about the belief, confession, repentance, and submission that are required to obtain salvation, and that those who refuse to come to Him in this way will bear the punishment for their sins. His mercy and longsuffering must be held in tension with His perfect justice and holiness.

ESSENTIAL #9: FERVENT *and* RIGHTEOUS

And yet God suffered long with them, waiting approximately two hundred years before relegating them to exile at the hands of the Assyrians in 721 BC. He sent them many prophetic warnings in the meantime, all with the intention of producing a repentant response.

One of His warnings to Israel along the way was this very drought that James highlights. We can see God's heart and purpose in the details of this judgment. Israel had moved away from the worship of the one true God, embracing the worship of other deities, particularly Baal. Baal was commonly worshiped by other people in the Canaanite region who believed he was seen in thunderstorms and worshiped him as the god of fertility.[41] The people of Israel began to look to Baal for rains in due season and bountiful harvests.

There's even more insight gathered from the name Baal. James Newell writes,

> Baal occurs in the OT as a noun meaning "lord, owner, possessor, or husband"... the noun comes from a verb that means to marry or rule over.[42]

Baal's very name implies that Israel had turned to a new lord and new husband. Doesn't that make Hosea's message to the northern kingdom make a little more sense?

With this in mind, we see a very clear purpose behind God's judgment. He wasn't simply punishing Israel for choosing another god, acting randomly out of scorn, spite, or jealousy. The drought sent a specific message to the people of Israel: "I am the One who gives you rain in its season and blesses your crops. I am the God of your produce and fertility. Your Baal is a worthless, dead idol." The goal was to shake them from their deception and give them the opportunity to return.

This drought came to a climax on Mount Carmel, where God explicitly demonstrated what the drought had implied, asserting Himself as the true God over Baal (1 Kings 18). Once the message had been

---

[41] James Newell, "Baal," *Holman Illustrated Bible Dictionary* (Nashville, TN: Holman Bible Publisher, 2003).
[42] Ibid.

received and many had responded, even though the repentance was short-lived, God ended the drought and sent the rains at Elijah's request.

This same principle was at work in the ten plagues of the Exodus. They weren't random punitive acts of anger but clear demonstrations of God's power over the various Egyptian gods in their very realms of power and influence. He did this to convince the Hebrews that He was superior to all the gods of the Egyptians, so they would willingly come out of Egypt and become the special possession, kingdom of priests, and holy nation He desired them to be.

Here's the point. When God allows bad things to happen—natural disasters, tragedies, even pandemics—it's not arbitrary but purposeful. The accuser would tell us that God is indiscriminately punishing people (or disengaged, or non-existent), but the real goal is for people to witness the events, consider eternity, and return to Him in repentance. And many do.

We can see this purpose even in Revelation. After the seven seals are broken and six of the seven trumpets sound, John appears to pause and take stock of what had transpired to that point:

> But the people who did not die in these plagues *still refused to repent* of their evil deeds and turn to God. They continued to worship demons and idols made of gold, silver, bronze, stone, and wood—idols that can neither see nor hear nor walk! And *they did not repent* of their murders or their witchcraft or their sexual immorality or their thefts. (Revelation 9:20–21, NLT, emphasis added)

Even in the seal and trumpet judgments of Revelation, the primary purpose is not punishment but warnings intended to cause people to repent.

We find it very easy to question God's heart when we consider His judgments. Have you noticed that on one hand we can be offended that God isn't doing more to address injustice in the earth, but on the other hand offended when He does address it?

Habakkuk wrestled with the same conundrum. He accused God of standing idly by while Judah descended into a culture of destruction, violence, and injustice (Habakkuk 1:2–4).

When God informed him that He was aware of Judah's issues and was already at work to address them, Habakkuk had a new problem: God was raising up the Babylonians to judge Judah (Habakkuk 1:5–11). This idea was deeply offensive to Habakkuk, as he considered the Babylonians to be more wicked than Judah. He was essentially saying, "God, aren't You taking this a little too far?" (Habakkuk 1:13).

Fortunately, Habakkuk gave us a wonderful example of how to respond in this dilemma: *"I will climb up to my watchtower and stand at my guardpost. There I will wait to see what the Lord says and how he will answer my complaint"* (Habakkuk 2:1, NLT). Do you see his posture? He was saying, "God, I don't see how this could possibly make sense. It doesn't seem like something You would do. But I'm going to stay here and wait until You make it clear to me."

Like Habakkuk, we need to understand that God is God and trust His perfect wisdom and unfailing love. When we do ask questions, we should take care not to ask them rhetorically, firing them off as an accusation. "How could You, God?" Instead we should ask and then wait for the response. And if a response doesn't come, we have a choice: trust our own understanding and feelings or trust that God is who He says He is (Hebrews 11:6, Proverbs 3:5–6).[43]

We often don't understand what God is up to when it comes to temporal judgments. Left to our own understanding, we can conclude that His judgments are too harsh.[44] But the Word tells us that God takes no delight in the death of the wicked, desiring that each one would turn from their evil ways (Ezekiel 18:23, 32, 33:11). Just like we saw in Revelation 9, perhaps His judgments are designed to get the attention of scores of people, bringing eternity to mind.

---

[43] For a fuller treatment of Habakkuk's dilemma, I recommend Samuel Whitefield's book, *Have You Been Blinded?* (Grandview, MO: OneKing Publishing, 2020).

[44] It's really important to note that not every disaster or tragedy is a judgment. Most are simply the cause and effect of people's choices. This includes everything from a senseless crime in a small neighbourhood to disastrous weather patterns influenced by our changing climate. We'll never be able to fully sort out what is what. But we can know, and trust, His heart and intentions behind it all.

We've already mentioned Isaiah 55:9 a couple of times. His ways and thoughts are higher than ours. Isaiah uses the analogy of the distance between heaven and earth—*"as the heavens are higher than the earth"*—to describe the chasm between His understanding and ours.

The other times we see that analogy employed in Scripture, it is used to describe the expanse of His lovingkindness (Psalm 103:11) and the unsearchable nature of the heart of a king (Proverbs 25:3). The greatness of His wisdom is only rivalled by His love, and vice versa. And they work together.[45]

In other words, His purpose is always redemptive. Just because we don't see it clearly, with our limited understanding and wisdom, doesn't mean it isn't there. Until the final trumpet, Christ's return, and the great white throne judgment, God sparingly allows and uses tragedies to shake mankind out of complacency and apostasy, with the intent that they would voluntarily return to Him.

Let's consider one final thought from the drought in Elijah's day. Though the prophet declared the drought in the land, he wasn't entirely exempt from it. Yes, the Lord miraculously provided bread and meat for him by way of ravens, as he hid near a brook east of the Jordan. He was sustained, but he didn't live comfortably. In time, the brook itself dried up and Elijah found himself on the move, settling for a while in Zarephath, as mentioned earlier (1 Kings 17).

Though God supernaturally provided for Elijah through that season, his life was greatly affected by the drought. It changed his normal diet and way of life. He was displaced and forced to move twice. While we're not told this, we can assume he had friends and family who struggled mightily, perhaps losing their lives, because of that very drought he had pronounced.

This didn't only happen to Elijah. Jeremiah was greatly impacted by the Babylonian destruction he had prophesied. Ezekiel and Daniel were taken into exile where they spent the rest of their days. Even Jesus Himself lived and was crucified under the shadow of Roman rule. If we think bad things will only happen to so-called bad people, we are mistaken (Luke 13:1–5).

---

[45] I am referencing the English Standard Version. Other translations use the phrase in other spots, but they're always used to describe His love, wisdom, ways, and judgments.

Peter, in fact, issues a clear warning along these lines, saying that judgment begins with the household of God and then continues to the disobedient (1 Peter 4:17). Paul argues that we are no longer destined for wrath because of the finished work of the cross (1 Thessalonians 5:9). So we know this isn't talking about eternal judgment.

But it does fit with what Jesus taught us about judging one another in the Sermon on the Mount. He wants us to be concerned with making sure we're in the clear before passing judgment on others (Matthew 7:1–5). In the same way, if we hope to see wickedness judged in our land, we must remember that it means He's going to deal with any lingering unrighteousness in us, His people, first (Malachi 3:1–5, 1 Peter 4:17). If we're going to ask Him to deal with sin and unrighteousness in the world, we better be ready for Him to deal with it in us.

What am I getting at with all this? My appeal is that we shouldn't be eager or flippant about praying for God to move in judgment against our leaders or nation. We need a great deal of humility and sobriety when it comes to this matter. Any shakings that would occur here would certainly touch our own lives. Are we prepared for that? We would do well to doublecheck our motives.

Do we want to see God move in judgment because it will prove that we're right? Have we been hurt or offended? Do we want to see our offenders pay for it? Or is our heart's desire truly that God use the absolute least severe means necessary to turn the greatest number of hearts?

As I hope you've seen from the book of James, the motives behind our prayers really matter to God.

Please hear my heart on these matters. I'm not going so far as to say that believers should never make decrees against darkness, or never pray for God to judge sin. What I am saying is that those types of prayers are clearly the exception and not the rule. Effective prayer comes from following His lead and pattern, not reacting to our wants or feelings.

The rule, or encouraged pattern of prayer in the Word, involves communicating directly with God and agreeing with His plans and purposes. Those plans and purposes are primarily the glorification of Jesus and the advancement of His Kingdom.

We know that He has established His church, and that the church is predestined to be an overcoming and victorious church (Matthew 16:18, Romans 8:35–39, 16:20, Revelation 12:11, 20:4–6). Our mindset in prayer shouldn't be limited to defending or protecting what we have but focused on seeing the Kingdom of God take more and more ground. What is the best way to drive out darkness? Bring in the light!

RIGHTEOUSNESS AND PRAYER

While James pointed to Elijah as an example of praying fervently, his primary point is that prayer is most effective when it flows from a life of righteousness. It's the prayer of a righteous man that accomplishes much.

> For the eyes of the Lord are on *the righteous*, and his ears are open to *their* prayer. (1 Peter 3:12, emphasis added)

As we saw earlier in Psalms 15 and 24, the effectiveness of our prayer lives is heavily influenced by what happens before we enter our prayer closets. The key is walking in righteousness.

An appropriate follow-up question might be: "Well, how do we do that?"

Righteousness doesn't necessarily mean sinlessness. A plain reading of the New Testament shows us that no one is perfect. Even the apostle Paul, who wrote more of the New Testament under the inspiration of the Spirit than any other man, plainly struggled with sinful desires and weaknesses (Romans 7:7–25). Peter, who was part of Jesus' inner circle, saw Jesus transfigured on the mountain, saw Him in His resurrected body, and was the primary human conduit through whom the Holy Spirit was poured out on both Jew and Gentile—but even he had to be rebuked and corrected for hypocrisy in his ministry (Galatians 2:11–14). He wasn't sinless.

Still, we know that the prayers of these men were effective and accomplished much. They moved in signs and wonders and saw much fruit from their life's work. They were righteous, though they were not sinless.

The biblical idea of righteousness is the idea of being in right standing, both with God and our fellow man. We are obviously dependent on Christ's imparted righteousness before God, but our journey as believers is about learning to walk in that righteousness.

We could deduce that James measures righteousness by the good works that flow from our faith (James 2:24). In other words, our righteousness is demonstrated in the fruit produced by our lives.

In John 15, Jesus taught His disciples the importance of abiding in Him. In His words we see two clear outcomes of this abiding. The people would bear much fruit and routinely see answers to prayer (John 15:5, 7). Jesus linked the good fruit of righteousness with answered prayer, both of which come from abiding in Him.

When we read a little further, we find out how to abide in Him: by keeping His commandments (John 15:10).

Willing obedience is what He looks for. Not perfection, but a heart that delights and desires to do His will (Psalm 40:6–8). Jesus became a man like us, in part so He could sympathize with us in our weakness. He knows our weaknesses and struggles, but He doesn't define us by them or hold them against us (Hebrews 2:17–18, Romans 4:7–8, Psalm 32:1–2, 103:6–14).

Even though Peter denied Jesus three times—after being warned that he would!—Jesus took the time in John 21 to intimately address Peter's failure in such a way as to restore him. Jesus saw Peter's willing spirit through the failure of his flesh and declared Him qualified to continue in his calling. Peter didn't have sinless perfection, but he did have a willing spirit.

Jesus sees when we have a willing spirit, even when it's overshadowed by the weakness of our flesh. If Jesus had been mostly concerned with Peter's ability to follow, Peter would have been disqualified. But Jesus looks for our willingness to follow.[46]

---

[46] It's true that leaders are held to a higher standard and that certain sins disqualify a person from public ministry. That is a discussion for another place. Our focus here is on all believers' invitation to approach His throne, not public ministry.

The starting point of this righteous living is giving a weak yet sincere "yes" in our heart toward Jesus and His commands. As we keep saying yes and acknowledging our weakness before Him, thus repenting, we walk more and more in His grace, the very grace that empowers us to do the things our flesh cannot.

The promise of the Lord's ear being attuned to the righteous is what makes the entire book of James applicable to prayer. In his letter, James has given us several examples of what righteousness looks like in the life of a believer.

Let's remind ourselves of some of these traits:

- Living in a way that is mindful of eternity (James 1:2–4, 12–15, 5:1–11).
- Giving God first place in our thinking (James 1:5–8, 4:1–10).
- Being quick to listen, slow to speak, and slow to anger (James 1:19–20, 26, 3:13–17).
- Being doers of the Word, not just hearers (James 1:22–25, 2:1–26, 4:17).
- Showing no partiality and loving our neighbours as ourselves (James 2:1–26, 5:1–6).
- Actively serving the poor and downcast (James 1:27, 2:14–26, 5:1–6).
- Being self-controlled in speech, blessing instead of cursing (James 1:26, 3:1–12, 4:11–12, 5:12).
- Walking in meekness and humility (James 1:21, 3:13–18, 4:1–17, 5:1–11).

This is by no means an exhaustive list of what it looks like to live righteously, or to have a walk worthy of the Lord. The New Testament makes other statements that address conditions for effective prayer and issues more than a thousand imperatives. But it does seem as though the Holy Spirit is highlighting these topics from James in a unique way.

ESSENTIAL #9: FERVENT *and* RIGHTEOUS

He is calling us to live mindful of eternity and the hope to which we have been called, not as a means of escapism but as a source of power to stay faithful in the face of the culture.

He is calling us to single-minded devotion to Him, loving Him with all our heart, soul, mind, and strength.

He is calling us to be quicker to listen and slower to speak so our words don't arise from reaction or offence. We are to hold our tongues until we've aligned with what God has to say about the situation.

He is calling us to live lives that demonstrate the freedom and power of the gospel, so that our preaching wouldn't be empty.

He is calling us to resist the polarization that is so common today by loving our neighbours as ourselves, whatever camp that neighbour might be from.

He is calling us to take the lead in actively loving and serving the poor and downcast as we continue to seek Him in prayer.

He is calling us to the same standard of love and forgiveness He has shown us, loving and blessing those who would hate and revile us.

He is calling us to live and walk in the same meekness and humility He embodies, willing to take the lowest place, to prefer and serve others, and to keep a right perspective of who we are—nothing special in and of ourselves, yet utterly priceless and completely successful as His glorious inheritance and the object of His affection.

Effective prayer isn't so much about saying the right words in the right ways to get God to move. He is drawn to the prayers of those who live lifestyles of loving obedience, as weak as that obedience may sometimes be. He is drawn to prayers that come from those who display good fruit, both in good works and the fruit of the Spirit.

This all points to the idea that prayer is holistic. It's not one isolated part of our lives in God but is influenced by, and influences, every other part of our lives as well.

Most of these traits are worked out in interpersonal relationships. This is why it's so important for people of prayer to be connected to the body of Christ as a member of a local church.

First, the local church provides opportunities to engage in good works, such as serving the poor. It's much easier to do this as a group than on our own, as we can benefit from mutual encouragement in doing this alongside others, and we can make a greater impact in doing this as a body (Ecclesiastes 4:7–12). Sure, it's sometimes easier to work alone, but we can't make nearly the same impact as we can with a team.

Second, the fruit of the Spirit is fleshed out in the context of community and relationships. We cannot grow in patience apart from having our patience tested. Our maximum potential in kindness is very low if we isolate ourselves. Gentleness and self-control have lots of opportunity to develop when we walk with people who aren't exactly like us. It's very difficult to bear good fruit if we only walk alone.

I know that many have been hurt by the local church. Maybe that shouldn't surprise us. Jesus Himself was betrayed and deserted by His little church of twelve. But that didn't keep Him from engaging with them and loving them. Even when He knew they would betray and desert Him that very night, Jesus spent an intimate evening with His disciples, celebrating the Passover, washing their feet, and equipping their hearts to endure their own troubles and tribulation (John 13–17).

If you've been hurt by your local church, take those hurts to the Lord and deal with them (1 Peter 5:7). Though these wounds are internal, they can have the same effect as an external wound. If you suffer a large gash on your arm, tend to the wound: clean it and dress it so it can heal properly. If you don't, the wound will be susceptible to infection. Not only that, but you don't want to walk around bleeding on everything and everyone you meet.

In the same way, if we're wounded by a local church and just move on to another without tending to the wounds, we'll wind up bringing that mess into the next place we go. At some point, we have to stop and deal with the issue.

If you're a member or leader of a local church that has offended or wounded someone, whether intentionally or not, I implore you to do what you can to make it right. Swallow your pride and repent of the things you can repent of. Don't act like nothing happened. Do what you can to keep clean accounts.

The local church isn't composed of perfect people, but of weak and broken ones who have sincerely said yes to Jesus, just like us. They will make mistakes, and we will sometimes get hurt by those mistakes. But if we can learn to speak and act as those who have received mercy and contend for unity as we mature together in Christ, we'll benefit by growing in good works and the fruit of the Spirit. As we increase in good works and the fruit of the Spirit, we'll see an increase in the effectiveness of our prayer lives.

THE WHOLE POINT

James' entire message about prayer appears to boil down to this: prayer isn't an isolated part of the Christian life, not just something we do. It's deeply connected to our entire lives. As we saw in Isaiah 58 and Amos 5, we cannot do the religious stuff, such as prayer and fasting, without the justice stuff, such as feeding the poor and loving our neighbours, and expect God to hear and answer us. It is the prayer of a righteous person that is most effective.

This means that how I treat the poor affects my prayer life. How I respond when reviled affects my prayer life. How I talk about my prime minister affects my prayer life. How I think about myself compared to others affects my prayer life.

I think this is the idea Jesus was getting at when He said, *"If you ask me anything in my name, I will do it"* (John 14:14). Praying in His name doesn't mean that the words "in Jesus' name" are a golden ticket. This gets to the concept of being a representative. A representative speaks and acts on behalf of another. A good rep doesn't share their own views and opinions when on the job; they reflect the views and opinions of the one they speak for.

We pray in His name when we represent Him and His values, both in our actions and words. Actions, by way of living righteously. Words, by praying the inspired Word. We pray in His name when we pray what He is praying (Hebrews 7:25). And those prayers are most effective when the rest of our lives are consistent with those same values.

The Word tells us that living a life in line with His values is the pathway to joy (Psalm 45:7, 68:3, 97:11). But that also opens the door to a more fruitful prayer life, which Jesus said would also make our joy full (John 16:24). You may be surprised to hear this, but a combination of upright living and a fervent prayer life is a source of joy! (Psalm 16:11, Isaiah 56:7)

With that, let's close with a few scriptures that draw this connection between righteousness and effective prayer. My hope is that people of prayer from every denomination and stream would experience what Jesus told us is available: that we could know the joy of abiding in Him and regularly see answers to prayer (John 15:1–11, 16:23–24).

> But seek first the kingdom of God and his righteousness, and all these things will be added to you. (Matthew 6:33)

> ...and whatever we ask we receive from him, because we keep his commandments and do what pleases him. (1 John 3:22)

> Whatever you ask in my name, this I will do, that the Father may be glorified in the Son. If you ask me anything in my name, I will do it. "If you love me, you will keep my commandments." (John 14:13–15)

> Who shall ascend the hill of the Lord? And who shall stand in his holy place? He who has *clean hands and a pure heart,* who does not lift up his soul to what is false and does not swear deceitfully. *He will receive blessing from the Lord* and righteousness from the God of his salvation. (Psalm 24:3–5, emphasis added)

> *If* you take away the yoke from your midst, the pointing of the finger, and speaking wickedness, *if* you pour yourself out for the hungry and satisfy the desire of the afflicted, *then* shall your light rise in the darkness and your gloom be as the noonday. And the Lord will guide you continually and satisfy your desire... (Isaiah 58:9–11, emphasis added)

ESSENTIAL #9: FERVENT *and* RIGHTEOUS

We ask God to give you complete knowledge of his will and to give you spiritual wisdom and understanding. *Then the way you live will always honor and please the Lord, and your lives will produce every kind of good fruit.* All the while, you will grow as you learn to know God better and better. (Colossians 1:9b-10, NLT, emphasis added)

APPENDIX A

Main Points and Prayer Points

At the National House of Prayer, our heart is to see every church in Canada grow in their identity as a house of prayer. My hope is that this book has given you some good keys to help you move forward in prayer. After all, what good is a book about prayer if it doesn't help or stimulate you to pray?

The point of this appendix is twofold.

First, it is meant to give you some point-form takeaways from each chapter. These are bite-sized versions of the points so you can easily remember them.

Second, it will give you some starting points to help you build these nine essentials into your own prayer life. The Holy Spirit will undoubtedly move you into new applications of these points in prayer, so don't feel tied to these exact prayers and points. Again, they're meant to serve as a starting point.

Read on, and pray on!

ESSENTIAL #1: AN ETERNAL MINDSET

Main Points:

- Living while aware of eternity keeps our priorities straight and our treasure in the right place.
- Pray for wisdom and pray with confidence in His goodness—without any doubting.
- We want to become people of one thing: one thing we ask, one thing we do, one thing is needed—to grow in our experiential knowledge of Him.

Prayer Points:

- Pray for grace to live with an awareness of the brevity of life:

  So teach us to number our days that we may get a heart of wisdom. (Psalm 90:12)

- Pray that we wouldn't run from troubles and suffering but have the grace to endure them faithfully in light of eternity:

  Dear brothers and sisters, when troubles of any kind come your way, consider it an opportunity for great joy. For you know that when your faith is tested, your endurance has a chance to grow. So let it grow, for when your endurance is fully developed, you will be perfect and complete, needing nothing. (James 1:2–4, NLT)

- Set your mind on "things above":

  One thing have I asked of the Lord, that will I seek after: that I may dwell in the house of the Lord all the days of my life, to gaze upon the beauty of the Lord and to inquire in his temple. (Psalm 27:4)

APPENDIX A: MAIN POINTS *and* PRAYER POINTS

ESSENTIAL #2: A LISTENING HEART *in* PRAYER

Main Points:
- Learn to be quick to listen and slow to speak in your times of personal prayer.
- Live from a balance of the revelations of His holiness and everlasting love.
- True power comes from His words, not ours. Learn to agree with what He is saying.

Prayer Points:
- Pray that we would remember to approach God in awe and wonder:

> Guard your steps when you go to the house of God. To draw near to listen is better than to offer the sacrifice of fools… [do not be] hasty to utter a word before God, for God is in heaven and you are on earth. Therefore let your words be few. (Ecclesiastes 5:1–2)

> Be still, and know that I am God! I will be honored by every nation. I will be honored throughout the world. (Psalm 46:10, NLT)

- Pray that we would grow in experiential knowledge of His goodness and greatness:

> …that the God of our Lord Jesus Christ, the Father of glory, may give you the Spirit of wisdom and of revelation in the knowledge of him, having the eyes of your hearts enlightened, that you may know what is the hope to which he has called you, what are the riches of his glorious inheritance in the saints, and what is the immeasurable greatness of his power toward us who believe… (Ephesians 1:17–19b)

ESSENTIAL #3: BE SLOW *to* ANGER

Main Points:
- We are called to be as He is in the world, and He is slow to anger.
- When a Christian is angry, it's not guaranteed to be righteous anger. Learn to differentiate between what anger arises from righteousness and what anger arises from our own fears.
- The anger of man does not produce the righteousness of God.

Prayer Points:
- Pray that our pursuit of righteousness would be rooted in love, not anger:

    And it is my prayer that your love may abound more and more, with knowledge and all discernment, so that you may approve what is excellent, and so be pure and blameless for the day of Christ, filled with the fruit of righteousness that comes through Jesus Christ, to the glory and praise of God. (Philippians 1:9–11)

- Pray for grace to love our enemies and bless those who persecute us:

    But I say, love your enemies! Pray for those who persecute you! In that way, you will be acting as true children of your Father in heaven… But you are to be perfect, even as your Father in heaven is perfect. (Matthew 5:44–45, 48, NLT)

- Pray that we would abound in the fruit of the Spirit:

    But the fruit of the Spirit is love, joy, peace, patience, kindness, goodness, faithfulness, gentleness, self-control; against such things there is no law. (Galatians 5:22–23)

ESSENTIAL #4: PRAY *with* IMPARTIALITY

Main Points:
- We are called to be as He is in the world, and He is impartial.
- No political party represents the Kingdom of God. He establishes His Kingdom today through His people, not political parties.
- We love and pray for all people, including all those in positions of authority, regardless of whether or not we agree with them.

Prayer Points:
- Pray for elected officials and others in authority in your life. For example, parents, employers, and pastors:

> Give your love of justice to the king, O God, and righteousness to the king's son. Help him judge your people in the right way; let the poor always be treated fairly. (Psalm 72:1–2, NLT)

- Pray that God would raise up wise, discerning, godly counsellors like Joseph and Daniel:

> The king said to Daniel, "Truly, your God is the greatest of gods, the Lord over kings, a revealer of mysteries, for you have been able to reveal this secret." (Daniel 2:47, NLT)

- Pray that Christians would be more likely to build bridges, not burn them:

> If possible, so far as it depends on you, live peaceably with all. (Romans 12:18)

ESSENTIAL #5: MINISTER *to the* POOR

Main Points:
- Faith that produces no good works is dead.
- If we ignore the cries of the poor, He just might ignore our prayers.
- God's heart is moved toward those who love and help the poor.

Prayer Points:
- Pray that the church would have a renewed passion to love and serve the poor:

  And let us consider how to stir up one another to love and good works… (Hebrews 10:24)

- Pray that God would demonstrate His love and care for the poor with signs and wonders, in the name of Jesus, through the hands of His people:

  And now, Lord, look upon their threats and grant to your servants to continue to speak your word with all boldness, while you stretch out your hand to heal, and signs and wonders are performed through the name of your holy servant Jesus. (Acts 4:29–30)

- Pray that the church would add works of service to her prayer and fasting:

  Remove the heavy yoke of oppression. Stop pointing your finger and spreading vicious rumors! Feed the hungry, and help those in trouble. (Isaiah 58:9–10, NLT)

APPENDIX A: MAIN POINTS *and* PRAYER POINTS

ESSENTIAL #6: FRESHWATER SPEECH

Main Points:

- Our words are important: God hears them, relates to us by them, and will hold us accountable to them.
- Pray *for* the release of the Kingdom of God more than *against* the work of the enemy.
- Our fight is not against flesh and blood (people) but against the spirit of the age at work in the background.

Prayer Points:

- Pray blessings over people and leaders you have spoken poorly of in the past:

    ...pray for all people. Ask God to help them; intercede on their behalf, and give thanks for them. (1 Timothy 2:1, NLT)

- Pray to receive God's heart for those we see as enemies:

    He does not want anyone to be destroyed, but wants everyone to repent. (2 Peter 3:9, NLT)

- Pray for those who have been blinded by darkness, that they would see Him:

    ...that the God of our Lord Jesus Christ, the Father of glory, may give you the Spirit of wisdom and of revelation in the knowledge of him, having the eyes of your hearts enlightened... (Ephesians 1:17–18)

ESSENTIAL #7: HEAVENLY WISDOM

Main Points:
- Wisdom is not stubborn but willing to yield.
- Trust God to avenge you, where necessary. Always repay good for evil. You have been shown mercy, so show mercy to others.
- Peacemakers will reap a harvest of righteousness.

Prayer Points:
- Pray for grace to demonstrate wisdom, not argue about it:

    Who is wise and understanding among you? By his good conduct let him show his works in the meekness of wisdom. (James 3:13)

    Take my yoke upon you. Let me teach you, because I am humble and gentle at heart… (Matthew 11:29a, NLT)

- Pray for grace to be patient, being quick to listen and slow to speak:

    A fool gives full vent to his spirit, but a wise man quietly holds it back. (Proverbs 29:11)

- Pray for grace to prefer others before yourself:

    Love one another with brotherly affection. Outdo one another in showing honour. (Romans 12:10)

ESSENTIAL #8: HUMILITY

Main Points:
- God resists the proud but gives grace to the humble.
- Jesus earnestly desires that His Bride would be one, as He is with the Father.
- Repentance is a gift. It is the doorway through which we access the experience of His mercy and grace. Do not resist repentance.

Prayer Points:
- Pray for grace to be humble, as He is humble:

> You must have the same attitude that Christ Jesus had. Though he was God, he did not think of equality with God as something to cling to. Instead, he gave up his divine privileges; he took the humble position of a slave… he humbled himself in obedience to God and died a criminal's death on a cross. (Philippians 2:5–8, NLT)

- Pray for a powerful witness of brotherly love and unity in the wider church:

> I pray that they will all be one, just as you and I are one—as you are in me, Father, and I am in you. And may they be in us so that the world will believe you sent me. (John 17:21, NLT)

- Pray for reconciliation where relationships have been strained by disagreements:

> "Lord, how often will my brother sin against me, and I forgive him? As many as seven times?"
> Jesus said to him, "I do not say to you seven times, but seventy-seven times." (Matthew 18:21–22)

ESSENTIAL #9: FERVENT *and* RIGHTEOUS

Main Points:
- Fervent prayer isn't primarily about volume or enthusiasm, but endurance.
- God's ear is attuned to the prayer of righteous ones.
- God doesn't expect perfect performance, but He does look for loyal hearts that express love through obedience.

Prayer Points:
- Pray that our times of intimacy in His presence would translate into obedience:

    As the Father has loved me, so have I loved you. Abide in my love. If you keep my commandments, you will abide in my love, just as I have kept my Father's commandments and abide in his love. These things I have spoken to you, that my joy may be in you, and that your joy may be full. (John 15:9–11)

- Pray that we would know His will, so that we would walk in righteousness:

    …we have not ceased to pray for you, asking that you may be filled with the knowledge of his will in all spiritual wisdom and understanding, so as to walk in a manner worthy of the Lord, fully pleasing to him: bearing fruit in every good work and increasing in the knowledge of God… (Colossians 1:9–10)

- Keep praying!

    Rejoice always, pray without ceasing, give thanks in all circumstances; for this is the will of God in Christ Jesus for you. (1 Thessalonians 5:16–18)

APPENDIX B

NHOP and the Canopy of Prayer

The National House of Prayer exists to activate strategic prayer across Canada. It was founded in 2004 by Rob and Fran Parker and has served as an embassy for God in the Canadian capital city of Ottawa, Ontario.

For many years, prayer teams and praying individuals have come to NHOP from across the country to pray for our government and the purposes of God in our land. The key passage for NHOP has always been 1 Timothy 2:1–4:

> First of all, then, I urge that supplications, prayers, intercessions, and thanksgivings be made for all people, for kings and all who are in high positions, that we may lead a peaceful and quiet life, godly and dignified in every way. This is good, and it is pleasing in the sight of God our Savior, who desires all people to be saved and to come to the knowledge of the truth.

Rob and Fran stepped down from the leadership of NHOP on January 1, 2021, handing over the reins to Chris and Marilyn Byberg. While there has been a shift in leadership, the vision and core values of NHOP remain the same: to encourage believers across Canada to pray for all people, and to keep our finger on the pulse of the nation by simultaneously tracking with events in the church and on Parliament Hill.

The vision and core values remain the same, but our approach is expanding.

In 2021, NHOP launched the Canopy of Prayer initiative. Our objective is simple: to raise up active prayer teams to stand on guard in every federal electoral riding across the country; as of July 2024, there are 338 ridings. We still welcome and invite people from across the country to come and pray with us in Ottawa, but the need for active prayer in your riding is just as great!

Before coming to NHOP, Chris and Marilyn were challenged by the Lord to get involved with their local politicians. For five years, they volunteered, served, and prayed for their members of federal, provincial, and municipal government. At one point, Chris served as the constituency office manager for his MPP (Member of Provincial Parliament). This is when the vision for Canopy of Prayer started to take shape.

Most Canadians don't understand this, but the constituency office is a nonpartisan place. Members are prohibited from wearing their party's colours there. That's because the constituency office is all about serving the community. Whether or not you voted for your elected member, you have an equal right to approach your member and ask for help.

In Ottawa, politics are extremely partisan. If you've ever watched a session of question period, you know what that looks and sounds like.

But the constituency office is where the member serves the community. It's also where we can serve our elected member.

It has been said that you can only have influence where you have relationship. If we hope to influence government at any level, we must get involved by being present and building relationships. Form letters and emails don't move the needle much; most members' offices are bombarded with so many each day that they can't hope to possibly read them all. But a constituent who comes to the office, speaking respectfully, bringing words of encouragement, and blessing instead of angrily ranting over an issue? That gets their attention.

When we bring this up, the most common response is, "But my member is from the _____ Party. You're telling me to serve her?" And we say, "Yep, that's what we're encouraging you to do." Remember the chapter about impartiality?

In addition, volunteering or serving at the constituency office isn't like joining that member's political party. It's serving an elected official. More than that, it's serving the community in your riding.

We have received multiple testimonies from people who have done this, and it has produced wonderful results. When you genuinely seek to bless and serve others, a relationship is built and trust is established. We hear testimonies of people having opportunities to pray with their members and being asked to pray into specific challenges. When we come with a servant's heart and an intent to bless, doors are more likely to open than slam shut. But as with heavenly wisdom, it often takes time.

The Canopy of Prayer is all about encouraging prayer and engagement in every riding across the country. We do this in a few ways.

NHOP School of Prayer. We are building a curriculum of prayer training for our Canopy of Prayer team members. As of now, we teach one track in the spring and one in the fall. Sessions are hosted on Zoom, and recordings and notes are shared for those who aren't able to participate in the live call.

This book was born out of one such track. Our School of Prayer is designed to help train and equip you to pray effectively for your community, city, province, and nation.

Prayer Stream. We send weekly e-newsletter updates with information on what's happening around the nation, with accompanying points to help you pray on these topics. More than just praying into the specific events that are unfolding, we want to pray for the hearts of the people who are driving these events as well as the people who are impacted by them.

Networking. We will help you link up with other Canopy members from your riding. Unfortunately, it's rare for local churches to have a robust community of prayer (we know the Lord is working on that). The Canopy of Prayer is a way to help you connect with praying people from other churches in your area, which can encourage you to remain fervent in prayer and build toward John 17 unity. There is the potential for friendships to be gained and greater impact to be had for the Kingdom in your area.

For more information about NHOP's Canopy of Prayer, please visit: www.nhop.ca. There you can find links to enroll in the Canopy of Prayer, subscribe to our Prayer Stream newsletter, and find information about the history of the NHOP. To inquire about inviting members of the NHOP team to preach or teach about prayer in your area, please email info@nhop.ca.

www.ingramcontent.com/pod-product-compliance
Lightning Source LLC
LaVergne TN
LVHW041542070426
835507LV00011B/877